THE
RIDING
INSTRUCTOR'S
~ HANDBOOK ~

THE
RIDING
INSTRUCTOR'S
~ HANDBOOK ~

Monty Mortimer

DAVID & CHARLES

A DAVID & CHARLES BOOK

First published 1981
Reprinted 1983, 1984, 1985, 1987, 1989, 1991
First published in paperback 1997

A catalogue record for this book is available from the British Library.

ISBN 0 7153 0622 7

Printed in England by Redwood Books, Trowbridge
for David & Charles
Brunel House Newton Abbot Devon

CONTENTS

FOREWORD

The survival of all species is dependent on the instinct to follow the example and teaching of others. Fortunately for mankind the desire to share one's knowledge and ability is almost universal. It is after all a form of immortality.

Books in their thousands are at hand to cater for this inborn need to acquire knowledge but, certainly in the equestrian world, it is rare if not unique to find one which specialises in *how* not *what* to teach. Major Mortimer's book does this admirably. His clarity of thought and attention to detail are supported by a simple, well written text and excellent illustrations. There is also a very refreshing lack of bias towards any particular method or school of thought.

But for me, its greatest value lies not in the written word but in the dedication and deep love of teaching which slowly becomes apparent between the lines. Without this, however great one's knowledge and riding ability, the 'gift' of teaching will never be bestowed.

SHEILA INDERWICK

INTRODUCTION

Having taught a wide range of subjects for some twenty-five years, it occurred to me that very little has been written on how to actually teach a particular skill or theory. I have therefore tried, in this short work, to suggest ways in which those of you who are so devoted to your subject that you wish to share it with others by teaching, may achieve your aim with the greatest effect.

Many volumes have been written on the horse and how it should be ridden, and this book is not intended to be added to that list. Where I have strayed into the subject of equitation or horsemastership it is intended only to assist the riding instructor in teaching his subject.

The rider has been referred to throughout the book as 'he'. This is not due to any chauvinistic prejudice but to avoid the rather cumbersome, continual reference to 'he/she'.

The riding instructor is generally thought to be one who teaches people to ride horses. To do this he has to depend very largely on the goodwill of his staunch friend and assistant, the horse. Ideally we would have a pool of correctly trained horses on which we would train novice riders, and a pool of expert riders who would train our young horses. This Utopian situation is unlikely ever to be achieved.

It is, however, impossible to separate the training of the rider from the training of the horse. Except in the very early stages of teaching the novice rider, where a trained horse has to be used, the instructor will usually find himself teaching a novice rider on a novice horse. Under these circumstances, as the rider improves so the horse will follow, and it is with this situation in mind that this book has been written.

For many years we have benefited from the very high standard of riding instruction that was maintained in the world's major cavalry schools, but we are now sadly coming to the end of the expert instructors trained by those schools. The responsibility for training riding instructors has now passed to civilian riding schools, and the various national bodies whose task is to guide and protect the interests of horses and riders. Their teaching principles are largely based on those of their military predecessors, as are those advocated in this book.

Many roads lead to Rome and it is stressed that the route suggested here is by no means the only one. It has been thoroughly tried and it works; it is therefore humbly offered for consideration by anyone who is setting out to teach this fascinating subject.

MONTY MORTIMER

1

THE QUALITIES OF A
GOOD INSTRUCTOR

'Those who can, do, and those who can't, teach.'
Whilst this comment is sometimes made by the cynic,
it does not follow that an expert on any subject
will necessarily be able to pass on his knowledge or
skill to others.

Many expert teachers are, however, failed or disappointed competitors, who, although in no way lacking in enthusiasm, have through lack of funds, opportunity or ability, failed to make the grade in their chosen sport.

Whilst to be a national or Olympic champion or an international competitor is sure to enhance the reputation of an instructor, these qualities do not necessarily make a good teacher. There are many other qualities which contribute to making a successful instructor.

KNOWLEDGE OF HIS SUBJECT

His knowledge must be sound and in considerable depth and detail. The complete instructor will have studied his subject and discussed it minutely with his fellow teachers. In order to have complete confidence in the doctrine that he is trying to put across to his pupils he must have dissected it, taken it apart and questioned it from every angle. Only in this way will he remove that which is irrelevant, untrue or just 'an old wives' tale', so many examples of which flourish in the riding world.

His teaching will be under scrutiny from his pupils and often from his fellows; so whilst he should never be over-dogmatic or unbending, the ability to defend his principles from a firm base of study and from detailed consideration of the facts is vital.

It is important that the instructor has a wide and detailed knowledge of schools of teaching other than his own. Only with this knowledge will he be able to justify his theories in relation to the theories of others. If he is vigorously opposed to any movement or exercise he should know quite clearly why he objects to it, and equally clearly why it is practised so widely and successfully by other trainers. Only with this depth of prepared and analysed knowledge will he be able to teach with confidence.

ESSENTIAL CHARACTERISTICS

Confidence

A riding instructor's pupils will often be nervous; his confidence will help to overcome their nervousness. Confidence will come with experience, but depends upon several things: his own ability to teach; his thorough knowledge of his subject and how to teach it; his own expertise as a performer in any required skills; and the preparation and planning of his lesson.

Enthusiasm

The good instructor must 'sell' his subject. His attitude should be rather like a salesman earning his pay on commission. Enthusiasm is infectious, and the instructor's enthusiasm will soon be imparted to his class.

Many instructors will teach several classes each day, and it is reasonable to assume that their enthusiasm will wane towards the end of the day. It must be remembered though that each new class of pupils starts fresh and expects a cheerful, enthusiastic teacher. They may not know, or even care, that he is taking his fifth or sixth class that day. They are, after all, paying for their instruction and deserve and expect enthusiastic teaching.

Manner

The instructor's manner must always be bold and confident, and his appearance is of vital importance. It is only good manners to appear before the class properly dressed in riding clothes. The pupils should notice the shine on his boots, and that his breeches, jacket, collar and tie are clean and well fitting. While it is usual for an instructor to wear a hat, men need not necessarily teach in a hard hat but lady instructors usually do. The instructor should always wear gloves and carry a riding whip. A slovenly appearance usually leads to slack instruction and a poor class reaction.

Instructors are sometimes seen smoking, leaning against the kicking boards of the school or even drinking their coffee whilst teaching. These are all aspects of an unacceptable manner in the riding instructor.

Using the voice

The use of the voice is an aspect of teaching which is often neglected: it must be clear and loud enough to be heard by all the pupils in the class, although this is difficult for some people to achieve without shouting. Lady instructors sometimes find this harder to achieve than men, but it can be done. It is not so offensive to the ear to hear a man shout an instruction but it always grates to hear a lady do so. There are, however, many very successful lady instructors who manage to make themselves heard in a clear and charming way.

The tone of the voice is important, and whilst to instruct in monotones can sound very boring, too much of a 'singsong' voice can be distracting. The instructor must therefore strive to find the happy medium of speed, pitch and tone. It is often very revealing to record one's own voice on tape whilst teaching; on playing the tape back, many instructors would learn a lot about the way they teach.

Riding training is usually carried out at a distance, and it is often difficult for an instructor to make himself heard and understood. Clear diction and well chosen words will help, and whilst instructions must be given in a commanding way, they must not sound like parade ground drill orders. The instructor's tone of voice must be encouraging and must never show any sign of exasperation or loss of temper.

Above all an instructor must avoid a nagging or complaining tone of voice.

Patience and understanding

To teach any subject the instructor requires considerable patience, and the ability to understand his pupils' problems. Most instructors will be passionately keen on their subject. When teaching riding the instructor must be able to assess his pupils' ambitions and limitations, both natural and self-imposed. Not every rider will have Olympic aspirations, but will be happy to hack out safely on a trained horse. The understanding instructor will appreciate this, and will modify his teaching accordingly. Similarly he will be able to cater for the competition rider who is striving for ever greater goals.

The good instructor will quickly identify the nervous rider or the rider whose conformation prevents him from achieving the correct riding position or application of the aids. It is sometimes difficult to understand how one student can find rising trot so difficult, or how another finds mounting such a task, but it is the duty of the good instructor to put himself in the position of these riders and so, taking their background and physical make-up into consideration, find the answer. This sort of challenge is what makes the teaching of any subject so fascinating and rewarding.

A sense of humour

There are very few professions in which a sense of humour is not an immense asset. People ride horses mainly for enjoyment, and this can be increased by an instructor who has a good sense of humour. In fact, it is safe to say that a riding instructor who does not have a fairly highly developed sense of fun is destined to a dull and frustrating career. However, care must be taken not to be facetious or sarcastic, and whilst every student of riding must learn to tolerate mild leg-pulling from his instructor, the age and personality of the teacher will dictate how far this can be carried.

THE INSTRUCTOR/STUDENT RELATIONSHIP

The instructor must set the standards that will determine the relationship that is to exist between him and his pupils. He should learn each pupil's background, and be quick to appreciate each individual's physical and mental limitations and difficulties.

Apart from the entirely aesthetic importance of correct riding dress, it is difficult to make progress in riding without the correct clothing, and the instructor must set the necessary standard. By his own good example, he will establish a standard in his pupils which will be both of help to them and a credit to him. It is unreasonable to expect a complete beginner to appear for his first lesson correctly dressed for riding. However, he must wear, apart from his normal clothes, sensible shoes, gloves and a hard hat at the appropriate BSI standard.

Whilst it is of great importance that there is communication in both directions between the instructor and pupil, progress is best made if the instructor gives commands and the pupil diligently and enthusiastically tries to carry them out. Throughout the lesson, whether it be as a class or to an individual, the instructor must make a break where he gives his pupils the opportunity to ask questions. Where these are not forthcoming, as is often the case, he must stimulate useful discussion by putting relevant questions to the class to confirm whether or not his teaching has been successful.

The instructor must establish his own reputation and credibility by teaching with sincerity and sympathy; he must be demanding and yet understanding, and above all he must realise his pupils' ambitions and limitations. For some students, riding is just for fun and exercise, and these pupils must be catered for because they contribute an important part to the riding school economy – and often, under the right instructor, they change their attitude and aspire to become serious horsemen.

For the serious student of classical equitation, or for the ambitious competitor, no demand from the instructor, within the student's immediate limitations at that time, is too great. For this student, absolute perfection must be considered as only just good enough.

2

TEACHING THE BEGINNER

The rider's first few lessons are usually designed to overcome a combination of the following factors: fear, ignorance of riding, lack of physical fitness and a general lack of understanding of the horse.

Fear is best overcome by the provision of the correct horse. It must of course be placid, quiet and used to being ridden by novices. It must stand still whilst being mounted and dismounted, but must also respond to the rider's aids and trainer's voice. Once a beginner rider has established a rapport with, and is confident in a particular horse, it is very much to his advantage to be allowed to ride that horse at each lesson until his confidence is such that he can go on to greater things.

The quiet, confident and friendly attitude of the instructor will help to allay the rider's fears, as will a quiet training area or riding school free from distractions or any sort of alarm. It is a disaster for any beginner rider to fall off his horse or to be run away with. Should either of these situations arise, the instructor must question his training methods closely in an attempt to discover where the fault lies. It is very often due to an unsuitable horse being provided, or the rider being asked to perform an exercise for which he is not ready. One thing is certain, however, that a mishap of this sort can only be a setback in the training of a novice rider.

Fear is not always overcome by improving the pupil's familiarity with the horse, but tasks such as saddling up, mucking out and grooming will improve his confidence in the horse in general which will, hopefully, be reflected in his riding.

Ignorance can be a problem where beginner riders come from

the city centre or suburbs, as they are currently doing in increasing numbers, and who probably have no knowledge of large animals. It is sometimes difficult for those of us who have spent many years with horses to understand how the uninitiated can have such a lack of understanding. The beginner rider so often compares horse riding with driving, and cannot understand why the accelerator, brakes and steering on his horse do not work as reliably as they do in his car. Nor does it probably occur to him how simple careless actions around the horse can have disastrous results: leaving the stable door open, taking the reins over the horse's head and letting them drop on the ground, or landing in the saddle with a thump when mounting are typical small points of basic instruction which the experienced rider would take for granted, but which no instructor can assume will be taken for granted by a beginner rider. For the sake of safety and progress, basic elements of simple horse-management must go hand in glove with riding training.

Riding, even in its simplest form, is physically demanding, and to the beginner, who may be tense and making unnecessary physical effort as a consequence, it is even more strenuous. People, as a rule, tend not to stand up straight, sit up straight, or carry themselves with good deportment. As soon as they start to ride, however, we ask them to sit in an upright position, with their bodies in a correct shape. Further, we ask them to sit astride the horse with their legs apart, making the joint where the top of the femur fits into the pelvis open sideways and forwards, and to maintain that position throughout their ride. This puts a strain on the muscles which control these joints in a way which the student has probably never experienced before. We then ask him to carry the toe a little higher than the heel, which may cause stiffening of the calf muscles. In short, the average beginner will not be fit enough to carry out the instructor's demands with regard to position for some time. The observant instructor will be conscious of this, and will take the rider's fitness into consideration when giving his instruction. Together with this must be considered the shape of the rider: some people have very round shoulders or short fat thighs, or are very tall or too fat, or have a combination of physical peculiarities which prevents them from attaining a classically perfect position. It is the duty of the riding instructor to achieve the best possible results that he can within the individual limitations of each rider.

THE FIRST LESSON

The best way to start off a beginner rider is on the lunge. In this way the horse is under the complete control of the instructor, and the student can concentrate on the development of his seat and position without being concerned with the control of the horse in any way. If the first lesson is taken as a class lesson with the pupils riding free, so many assistants are needed that individual private lessons would have been easier to run in the first place. Half an hour on the lunge will result in much more real progress being made than in a one-hour class lesson of first-time riders.

For the first lesson the horse should be dressed in a suitable saddle (not forward cut), neckstrap, snaffle bridle, side-reins, lungeing cavesson, lunge-rein and brushing boots. Having checked that the rider is suitably dressed, from a point of safety only, the instructor should show him how to lead the horse out of the loosebox and into the school. It is a good start for the student to do this on his first day.

The rules of the riding school must be taught and observed from the very beginning. These include knocking on the riding-school door (if it is an indoor manège) and asking for permission to enter, or whatever the local rule may be, and forming up correctly on the centre line to mount under control.

Correct mounting and dismounting should be taught at this stage, and it is of considerable importance to the rider, the horse and the saddle that this *is* done correctly. The competent instructor will never allow it to be carried out incorrectly. Mounting and dismounting on both the near- and off-sides must be taught, but the off-side will come later, as will mounting without stirrups. The instructor should demonstrate the correct way to mount and dismount, explaining what he is doing as he goes through the actions.

The practice of dismounting by throwing the right leg over the horse's withers and dropping to the ground should be forbidden: it is potentially dangerous, and is quickly picked up and copied by young riders. If it is allowed to become a habit, and if, one day, a horse does shy and take fright once the rider has dropped his reins and has got his right leg part-way over the horse's withers, the resulting fall could be very serious.

Skills are best taught by:

EXPLANATION
DEMONSTRATION
APPLICATION

Here the instructor explains and demonstrates at the same time. On occasions it will be found to be advantageous to demonstrate, then explain, and then allow the student to apply the teaching.

Once the rider is in the saddle he must be taught, quickly, how to hold both reins in one hand whilst he uses the other hand to adjust his stirrup leather, and then to change the reins to the opposite hand whilst he adjusts the other stirrup leather. A beginner rider must never be allowed to drop the reins whilst he uses both hands to adjust one stirrup leather, or to take his foot out of the stirrup iron. This is often seen, but it is incorrect, sloppy and potentially dangerous. If adjusting the stirrup leathers is taught correctly from the start it will not be long before the rider can adjust them quickly at halt or as he moves along without looking down, which is so necessary to the practical horseman. Having said that, this simple task is often made difficult by poorly kept saddles and stirrup leathers, leathers that are stiff or too thick for the stirrup bars, worn-out buckles, or pairs of leathers with holes that do not match. A combination of these factors can make stirrup adjustment difficult even for the most experienced rider.

When the stirrups have been adjusted correctly and the rider understands which way to put his foot into the stirrup iron

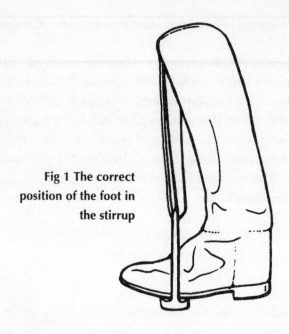

Fig 1 The correct position of the foot in the stirrup

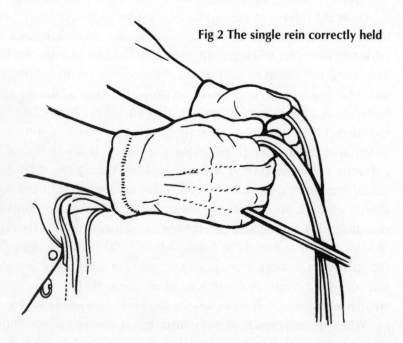

Fig 2 The single rein correctly held

without twisting the leather, he must be shown how to hold the reins even though he will not hold them at first whilst he is being lunged. Then, whilst still at halt, the instructor must go quickly through the correct position in the saddle. At this stage it is sufficient to get the rider to sit in the lowest part of the saddle and as straight as possible, and he should be shown which part of his foot should be on the stirrup.

Remember the student has come to *ride*, and as by now half the lesson time will have passed, he will be beginning to wonder how much of the lesson is administration, protocol and preparation, and how much is actual riding. The good instructor will know the importance of correct preparation, but he will also know how important it is to the pupil to get on with the job of riding as soon as possible. At this stage the reins should be taken from the rider, twisted under the horse's gullet and secured by the throat lash.

Fig 3 The reins safely secured before lungeing. Note the snug fit of the lunge cavesson

Figs 4 Three views of the correct seat

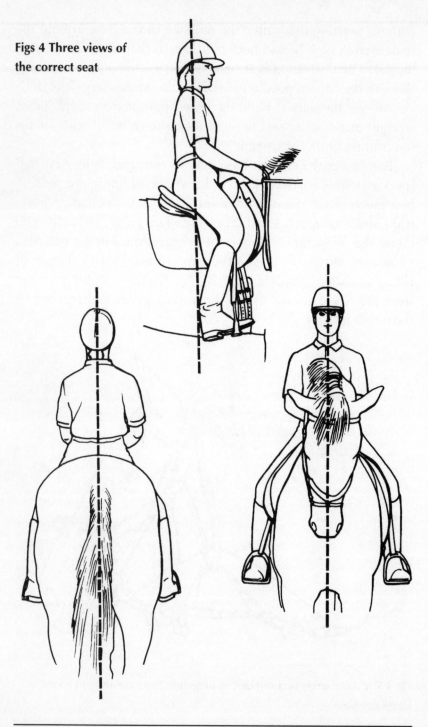

The student is asked to hold the pommel of the saddle by looping one or two fingers of each hand underneath it. The way in which the pommel is held is important, because if it is held incorrectly, the rider may push himself up and out of the saddle and not pull himself down and into the saddle which is the intention.

The horse and rider are now ready to be moved off into walk by the instructor, and it is important that the pupil is told what is going to happen. The instructor must explain that he is in control of the horse completely, and that the rider need do nothing but relax and try to carry out his instructions.

Once the horse is on the lunge circle in walk, the instructor can start to improve the rider's position. As so much time and effort is spent on achieving a correct riding position, the pupil should be told why it is so important, and this is as good a stage as any to do this. It will give the student 'the reason why' (an important aspect of all training), and it will give him something to think about and should help him to relax during these first few circles at walk. Thus it should be explained to him that there are three main reasons for achieving a correct position.

The first is that the horse was not designed to carry a rider on his back, and if we want him to perform well we should make the load that we ask him to carry as well balanced as possible. This will make the task of both horse and rider very much easier. It is often helpful to make an analogy to stress a point, and so we might make the comparison of carrying 6.8kg (15lb) of shopping home in two shopping baskets: it is much easier to carry if you have 3.3kg (7.5lb) in each basket, thus balancing the load, than if you have 2.2kg (5lb) in one basket and 4.5kg (10lb) in the other.

The second reason for sitting in the correct position is that the rider must be able to apply the aids with his legs, his seat and his hands quickly and effectively. This can best be achieved from sitting correctly in the saddle.

The third reason is that the rider should try to look as elegant as possible. The combination of horse and rider must be pleasing to the spectator's eye, and the classical correctness of the rider's position will play a major part in achieving this.

At this point in the rider's training the importance of suppleness and controlled relaxation must be mentioned. Tenseness and stiffness are equally disastrous in both horse and rider, and will be the result of apprehension and lack of confidence at this stage. It is therefore the instructor's first task to put the pupil at ease and to improve his confidence, and this is best done by getting him to carry out a series of exercises. When the instructor sees that the moment is right, he can ask the rider to let go of the saddle with his inside hand only, and rest that hand on his thigh. He can then ask him to stretch that arm out level with his shoulder, and to make large circles slowly backwards with the arm whilst keeping his shoulders square to the front. After five or six circles he should be told to rest, to hold the pommel with both hands again, and then to repeat the exercise with the outside arm. By now it will be time to change the rein, because to work equally on both reins is of vital importance if horse and rider are to progress in an even and balanced fashion.

Provided that this training has proceeded according to plan, the next exercise can be attempted. Here the rider is asked to let go of the saddle with both hands, and to rest them on his thighs. When he is seen to be confident and balanced, the instructor can ask him to stretch both arms out level with his shoulders and to make large circles slowly backwards with both arms. Care must be taken to see that he does not grip up with his knees, calves or heels when he lets go with both hands; it is a natural reaction, but it is clearly wrong. Part of the value of these exercises is that the rider should be able to isolate and exercise one part of the body whilst leaving the rest of it still and supple, and in the correct position.

There are many exercises that the imaginative instructor can introduce into this first lesson, some of which are particularly useful in correcting a particular fault. For example, where a rider persistently has trouble with the right shoulder coming in front of the left shoulder, a short session of work on the lunge can be beneficial, during which he should hold the pommel of the saddle

Fig 5 Exercises to improve suppleness on the lunge, moving one and then both arms in a full circle

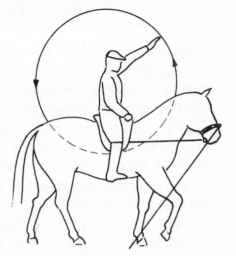

with his left hand and the cantle with his right.

Almost any exercise which will improve the rider's confidence, suppleness, agility and understanding is acceptable, provided that it is safe and will not create a problem later on in the rider's training.

If possible this first lesson should be completed with a circuit or two on each rein in sitting trot. It will give the rider an incentive, it will give him 'a look forward' to the next lesson and it will finish the lesson with a sense of real achievement. The rider must be given the opportunity to ask questions before he dismounts, and must be made to dismount properly, run up the stirrup

irons, loosen the girth and turn the horse in correctly. This is an extremely important aspect of all riding training.

In the interests of safety the side-reins should only be fitted to the bit whilst the horse is working. They should be detached from the bit and secured to the 'D' rings on the saddle whilst the horse is being led to and from the stable, and when the rider is mounting and dismounting.

The actual lungeing of the horse is discussed in Chapter 4.

THE SECOND LESSON

In this lesson the rider continues on the lunge. Once again he collects his horse from the stable and, under supervision, leads it into the school where he checks the girth and adjusts the stirrups. Most beginners of average physical fitness will be able to mount satisfactorily on their own, although there may be cases where the overweight, more elderly or less agile pupil will need a mounting block or a leg-up. Both these methods of mounting should be taught, if only in the interests of the horse's comfort and wear on the saddle.

Work on the lunge at this stage of training is vital, but it must be kept interesting and the pupil must not be allowed to feel that because he is not riding free he is not making progress. It would benefit the beginner rider greatly to keep him on the lunge for much longer than we usually do, and it is always an advantage even for an advanced rider to be trained on the lunge from time to time.

However desirable this may be, some practical considerations have to be taken into account: firstly, most trainee riders want to get on and ride on their own, and there is a chance that they will lose interest if they are kept on the lunge for too long; secondly, it must be more expensive for them to have private lunge lessons than to join a class; and thirdly, it is usually uneconomical from an instructor's point of view, as it is often not possible to charge a realistic fee for individual instruction.

This subject is raised here because it is from the second lesson onwards that the instructor must begin to ask himself 'When will this pupil be ready to join a novice class lesson?'

In this second lesson, work must start at walk again and the main points of the previous lesson revised. As soon as the exercises are mastered in walk and the rider is sitting in approximately the right position, then work must start in sitting trot. As his confidence improves he can be asked to make the arm-circling and trunk-twisting exercise in sitting trot, and the instructor must remember to make regular and frequent changes of rein.

Throughout this lesson the instructor must correct the rider's position, and should encourage him to sit deep in the lowest part of the saddle in a supple, upright way. He must be told to try to blend the movement of his body into the movements of the horse's back, and it should be made clear to him that he should not make more movement with his body than the horse makes for him.

The astute instructor will recognise the time when he can ask his pupil to take away the stirrups, which may well occur during the second lunge lesson. Whilst it is emphasised that this work on the lunge is done to get the rider in the correct position and sitting in the bottom of the saddle, his safety and confidence must be a prime consideration.

Where the use of stirrups on the lunge is concerned, there is a conflict of interests. It is clearly an advantage for the beginner to have the use of his stirrups to improve his safety and confidence, but it is a disadvantage if the rider learns to depend too often or too quickly on the stirrups for his security. A much deeper seat and a better feel for the movement of the horse will be built into the rider who is trained on the lunge without stirrups. However, common sense must prevail, and where the pupil is clearly nervous or is insufficiently fit or agile, he should be allowed to keep his stirrups for the first few sessions. The instructor at this stage can watch for the opportunity to introduce his student to rising trot. There is no set time for this, and the instructor should recognise when his student is ready. The rider who shows good co-ordination and is obviously comfortable and in harmony and balance with the lunge horse will sometimes make a few voluntary steps in rising trot without being asked to do so; this should be noticed by the instructor and encouraged. This is, however, not always the case, and the instructor must explain to his pupil what is required in rising trot. The pupil's attention should be drawn to a rider who is executing a good rising trot and the movement should be explained to him. He can then practise the movement a little at halt. This should not be overdone as it is difficult to do correctly, and the feeling is not quite the same as the up-and-down movement required at trot.

When practising trot on the lunge, the circle must be a little bigger, up to about 15m, and the horse must be sent on a touch faster and with rather more impulsion. It is difficult for a beginner to pick up rising trot if the pace is too slow or the impulsion insufficient. Rhythm plays a very important part in rising trot and a good rhythm is more likely to be achieved if the speed of the trot is good and the impulsion sufficient.

To introduce the rider to rising trot whilst he is holding the pommel of the saddle is a mistake as it creates a rather cramped and stiff feeling. It is preferable if he can carry his hands as though he were holding the reins, although if he becomes unbalanced, he can rest them on his thighs. Holding the neckstrap is a further alternative, but there is the danger here that he will learn to pull himself up by using the neckstrap and this could lead to pulling himself up with the reins. The disadvantages of this need no explanation.

The diagonal on which he is rising at this stage is of no importance, as this can be taught later. If it is introduced here it may only complicate what to some pupils is already a difficult exercise in co-ordination.

Both rider and instructor will have made good progress if by the end of the second lunge lesson they have carried out some useful gymnastic exercises at walk and sitting trot, have started to establish a correct rider's position, and have achieved a few circuits in rising trot.

Beginner riders come in all shapes and sizes. They will range from the unathletic, overweight person who may be in their teens, middle-aged or somewhere in between, to the fit, lithe, agile person who has played other games successfully and has good mind and muscle co-ordination.

The good instructor will quickly assess his pupil and know how much to ask from him. Some will thrive on being extended to their limits, others will have to be nursed very carefully, both physically and mentally, and there are many somewhere between these extremes. Half an hour is sufficient for the beginner's lunge lesson, and if he is made to work correctly this lesson can be very demanding physically. The horse must also be considered, as a half-hour lunge lesson in which he will probably work for twenty minutes will be plenty for him.

Whilst all riders will want to progress, the instructor must take care not to rush these first vital lessons. It should be remembered that 'haste is the enemy of perfection'.

THE THIRD LESSON

If normal, average progress has been achieved this should be the last of the beginner's lunge lessons. In the first two lessons we worked on establishing the correct basic position, and tried to build up the rider's confidence by giving him simple gymnastic exercises to do at halt, walk and sitting trot. Rising trot was then introduced.

In the third lesson the rider is taught how to hold the reins, and is made to ride holding them in walk and trot. Once this has been completed the instructor can explain the aids and how they are applied. At this stage he will be limited to the aids for the upward and downward transitions from halt through walk and trot back to halt. The aids to turn to the left and right can be explained here but obviously cannot be practised until the pupil is off the lunge.

The aids can now be put into effect by the rider to coincide with the instructor's commands to the horse. As the rider's aids improve and become more effective, so the instructor can reduce his commands to the horse until the rider is controlling it with his own aids although still on the lunge.

This lesson can be concluded by removing the lunge cavesson and side-reins and allowing the rider to ride loose in the school, practising progressive transitions from halt, through walk and trot and back down through walk to halt. As his confidence improves, the aids to turn and circle can be practised, and finally the rider will be ready to join a suitable class for his next lesson.

A few general points on teaching the absolute beginner might be made here: the correct riding position is of fundamental importance, and in the first lesson it was explained to the pupil why it is so important: in doing this, the words and expressions that the instructor chooses will have a direct effect for good or ill, and he must therefore consider the words he uses very carefully. Most students will do their very best to carry out the instructor's commands, some to such an extent that they try too hard, and this may have an adverse effect. The versatile instructor will therefore have a variety of expressions to achieve the same end: thus to persuade the rider to hold the upper part of his body in the correct position he can use a number of different phrases, such as 'Sit up straight', 'Square the shoulders', 'Shoulders back', 'Hollow the back', 'Close the shoulder blades', and many others which will have a similar result. Some of these, however, will have an adverse effect on some riders. For instance, to ask a rider to 'Square his shoulders' often results in him pulling his elbows behind his back and stiffening his neck and shoulders. Perhaps the best expressions to use in order to achieve the correct shape of the upper body are to ask him to 'Lift up the chest and put it out', or to 'Stretch the distance from the hip bone to the bottom rib long'; this makes the abdomen flat because it puts the upper part of the body into the required position without introducing any stiffness or tension.

There are many ways to ensure that the rider holds his head in a natural, controlled, relaxed position. One very good way to achieve this is to ask him to 'point his nose and his chin between the horse's ears and feel the back of his neck in the back of his collar'. He should be told that he can look down at his horse as much as he likes, but he must learn to look down along his nose, out of the bottom of his eyes and without tipping his head down.

Teaching the rider the correct way in which to hold the reins sometimes presents the instructor with a problem. It can be explained by likening the rein to a little bird held in the hand: if you hold it too tightly you will crush it, and if you hold it too loosely it will fly away. The snaffle rein is best held between the third and the little finger, although it may be held around the outside of the little finger. The hand should be closed sufficiently

Fig 6 The correct position of the hands/arms

to make a good contact between the hand and the rein, but not so tight that the knuckles go white and the muscles of the forearm become stiff.

The reins should be of equal length, with the hands the same height above the wither and an equal distance on either side of it. The thumbnail is towards the sky, with the knuckles to the outside.

When describing how the arms should be carried, it is very helpful to explain that there should be an imaginary straight line from the rider's elbow, through his little finger, to the bit. The top of the arm should be held close to the rider's side, not too closely but just allowing the inside of the sleeve to brush against the side of the jacket.

The use of an analogy is sometimes helpful. For example, the way the rider's leg should hang around the horse's side has been likened to 'a wet dishcloth flopped over the side of the kitchen sink'. This is a particularly imaginative comparison and can obtain exactly the right result in some cases.

The choice of the right words or expressions can be as useful and helpful as the choice of the wrong words can be harmful and misleading.

3

THE CLASS LESSON

Class lessons are useful because they provide an economical way of training a number of riders at the same time in a limited area. A good instructor will soon create an air of camaraderie in his class, a feeling that all his pupils have a common aim and that they are each confronted with similar problems.

To be successful, a class lesson should not contain more than eight pupils. A very experienced instructor may handle more, but the success of a larger class will depend on the degree of competence of the students and how capable they are of working on their own within the class. In any case, the more pupils there are, the less individual instruction each person will be given.

To control this class effectively the instructor will require a covered manège not less than 40m by 20m, or a fenced-in, outdoor arena of similar dimensions. A slightly larger school has obvious advantages, but a class of eight can be trained satisfactorily by a competent instructor in an area this size. The schooling area must be marked out with reference points (Fig 7): these are essential for the instructor to be able to command the ride effectively.

Ideally, a class ride should consist of riders of an equal or at least a very similar standard; if the standard within the ride varies too greatly it can be frustrating for the more advanced riders. The class does, of necessity, have to progress at the pace of the slowest pupil; and whilst even the most advanced rider should be prepared to work on and revise the basic principles, the frustration which may be caused in these circumstances must be appreciated.

The choice of horses for a class ride requires careful consideration. To have one or two horses that are onward bound and one or

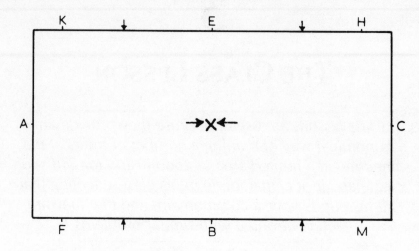

Fig 7 The riding school layout, showing the four circle points

two which get left behind can create difficulties in the class and detract from its efficiency to a great extent. It is therefore important that both riders and horses are of a uniform standard as far as possible. Furthermore, for a successful class lesson the practical instructor will arrange to have a trained rider as leading file. This precaution will serve two major purposes: firstly, he will be able to set a sure, steady, even pace at walk, trot and canter; and secondly, he will be able to demonstrate to the class when required to do so.

THE CLASS LESSON FORMAT

The object of a class lesson is to involve as many riders as possible in maximum activity, simultaneously and under control. (Note that the class being considered here is a class of novices; methods of teaching a class of more advanced riders will be considered later in this chapter.)

Most class lessons are programmed for one hour, and if the whole hour is used constructively it is sufficient for both horse and rider. At the start of the lesson the instructor must introduce himself to the class. This should be done if it is the first time that he has taught the class, or if any individual person has just joined them. It is only good manners and creates a better class spirit if the individual members of the class are introduced to one another, and this applies particularly to new members joining the class.

It is important that the instructor finds out about the standard of training of his pupils before the start of the lesson. If he waits until the beginning of the lesson he will not be able to plan his work, which will result in an 'off the cuff' air in his teaching.

The instructor should be quick to learn the students' names. It is unacceptable to refer to a student by his number in the ride (except on some special occasions, as described later) or by the name of the horse. Remembering names is difficult for some instructors, particularly when they are teaching several classes every day and may see some of their students only once a week. It is, however, a skill which has to be developed, and it will certainly impress and even flatter some students if the instructor can achieve it, especially as it may even offend those whose names have been forgotten.

Mounting up

Each member of the class should collect his horse from the stable and, under supervision, lead it correctly into the school to form up on the centre line. They should stand in a straight line with a safe distance between each horse, the student standing correctly at the horse's head with the stirrups down and the girth checked ready to mount. The instructor gives the word to mount, and supervises this carefully to see that it is carried out correctly by each member of the class. Once all are in the saddle, each member should be inspected to see that the tack is fitted correctly and that the girths are adjusted. At this stage, if necessary, the class can be taught how to adjust the girth when mounted.

The instructor must insist that each rider sits correctly in the saddle right from the start of the lesson; as he inspects them he has the opportunity to correct the way in which they are sitting. This will include ensuring that the rider has his foot in the correct side of the stirrup iron, a mistake often made by the beginner when mounting.

Once all the preliminaries have been completed, work can be started; the ride should never be left standing still for too long. It is bad for horses to be kept standing still with riders on their backs and both will soon get cold. Sufficient rest periods must of course be provided throughout the lesson for horse *and* rider, but at the start of the lesson one should proceed with the actual riding as soon as possible; after all, that is what the riders have come to do.

Moving off

The instructor must now give the command for the rider to move off. As they are on the centre line at rest, he may say, 'Take up your reins, correct the position – and walk, march; on reaching the track, left turn in single file'. There are several ways in which the commands can be given. The commands suggested throughout this book are recommended as being short, clear and precise. Each command must have a 'cautionary word of command' to warn and prepare the ride, followed by an 'executive word of command' on which the instruction is actually carried out.

At walk

The ride is now in walk on the left rein following a trained leading file who is setting a steady, even pace. Here the instructor explains that he wants each member of the ride to keep one horse's length from the next: this is for the sake of good order, and to prove to him that each rider is in control of his horse, and these facts must be explained to the class.

Once the riders are walking on at the correct distances, they must be taught how to ride through the corners of the school, making a quarter of a circle and going as far as possible into the corner without going so deep that they upset the horse's balance or spoil the pace. Frequent changes of rein must be made, and the simplest way to introduce this is for the class to ride across the diagonal from quarter marker to quarter marker (Fig 8, p39).

This initial period in walk serves to warm up both horses and riders, and the instructor must pay strict attention to warming up, particularly with unfit riders or when the weather is cold. He should also use this period to correct individual riders' positions and to teach the application of the aids. He should never address his remarks privately, to one person; he can refer to any individual, but he should speak so that the whole class can hear. Very often he will find that one member of his class requires more attention than the others, and great care must be taken here to ensure that this extra attention is not given at their expense.

At trot

When he is about to work the class in trot, the instructor must prepare them correctly. He must remind the class that the horses should be walking actively, and that the reins must be shortened a little so that they are the correct length when the horse is in trot. A suitable word of command here would be 'Prepare to trot rising – is your walk sufficiently active? – will your reins be the right length when you are trotting? – ride *ter-rot*.' The lengthening of the word 'trot' will be understood by the school horses and will help the riders with the transitions.

At a later stage this command can be reduced to 'Prepare to trot rising – ride trot'. If the school horses are very responsive to the instructor's words of command in transitions both up and down, he must do something to disguise his words of command lest the horses respond more quickly than the riders can apply the aids. This is often the case, and of course does not improve a rider's ability to give the aids. To overcome this problem the instructor could choose to say 'Prepare to trot rising – trot now': this might help to disguise his intention from the horse and put the onus entirely on the rider to make the transition by the correct application of the aids. Once the class is trotting, the instructor can work on improving each rider's position in rising trot.

Improving the rising trot is difficult for some riders. It must be explained to them that the shape of the body and the position of the legs and hands is exactly the same as in walk or sitting trot, the only difference being that the top part of the body is inclined slightly forward from the hips, and not from the waist, as this rounds the back.

The shoulders lead the movement and rise slightly over the hands. It is not a question of standing up and sitting down, but of lifting the seat out of the saddle and lowering it down again under control. It should also be made clear to the rider that if he sits in the correct position and is supple, the movement of the horse will throw him up sufficiently and that no real physical effort is required on his part. In fact, too much physical effort on the part of the rider will spoil the rising trot: all that he is required to do is to remain supple in the elbows and the shoulders so that his body can go up and down without moving his hands. He should lift his seat out of the saddle with his hips and shoulders parallel to the horse's shoulders, and lower the seat down onto the saddle again with equal weight on each seat bone. (This explanation is not intended to be a lesson in how the rising trot should be made, but rather to suggest to the instructor some ways in which he can put this subject over to his pupils.)

SCHOOL EXERCISES

There are many school exercises that can be made in both walk and trot; these are designed to enable the instructor to involve the whole class in maximum activity whilst keeping good control and making individual corrections to the riders. They should be carefully explained to the class, and practised first in walk and then in trot.

Changing the rein across the diagonal (Fig 8)
The command should be given as the leading file passes the F marker on the right rein: it is, 'In single file at K, right incline and change the rein through M.'

Changing the rein up the centre line (Fig 9)
The command is given as the leading file passes the E marker on the left rein: 'In single file, turn up the centre line at A and at C change the rein.'

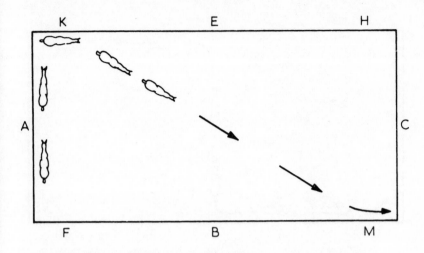

Fig 8 In single file at K right incline and change the rein through M

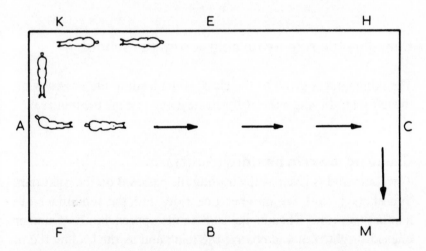

Fig 9 In single file turn up the centre line at A and change the rein at C

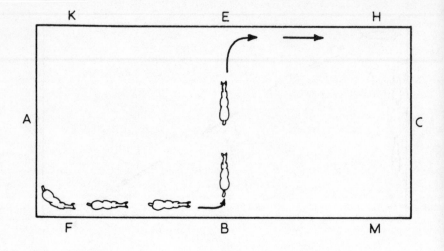

Fig 10 In single file at B turn left and change the rein at E

✳Changing the rein by turning across the school
(Fig 10)

The command is given to the class as the leading file passes A on the left rein: 'In single file at B, left turn and change the rein at E.'

✳Changing the rein by rides (Figs 11a, b)

The command is given as the leading file passes B on the right rein: 'Numbers 1 to 4 are number one ride, and the remainder are number two ride.' Then as the leading file approaches E: 'Number one ride, right turn and change the rein'; and as the leading file of number two ride approaches E: 'Number two ride, right turn and change the rein.'

This exercise will encourage precise, accurate riding as one ride. The riders must turn together and must ride across the school at right-angles, maintaining their spacing and dressing. The leading file of number two ride must not drift inwards to follow number one ride, but must continue straight down the long side of the school until he receives the command to turn.

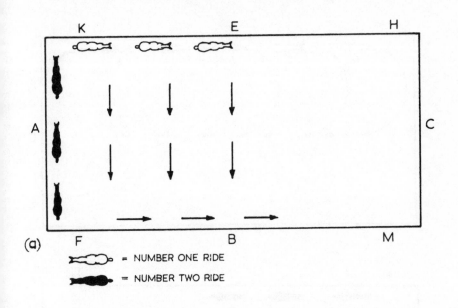

(a)

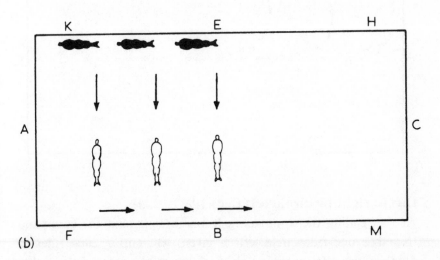

(b)

Fig 11 The two rides changing the rein: (a) Number 1 ride – right turn and change the rein; (b) Number 2 ride – right turn and change the rein

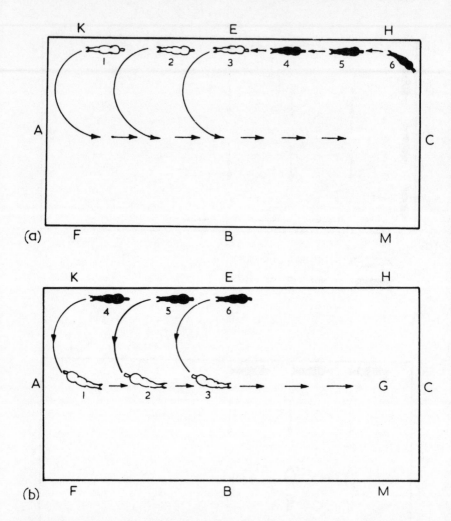

(a)

(b)

✳ Circle right or circle left (Figs 12a, b, c, d)

As the leading file approaches K on the left rein, the command 'Number one ride circle left' is given, whereupon each rider in number one ride makes a half circle on to the centre line so that number one ride forms a single file down the centre line towards C, with number 4 as leading file. As the first rider in number two ride approaches K the command is given, 'Number two ride circle left'. Number two ride performs the same exercise so that the whole ride is moving down the centre line in single file towards C. As the leading rider in number one ride approaches G the command is given,

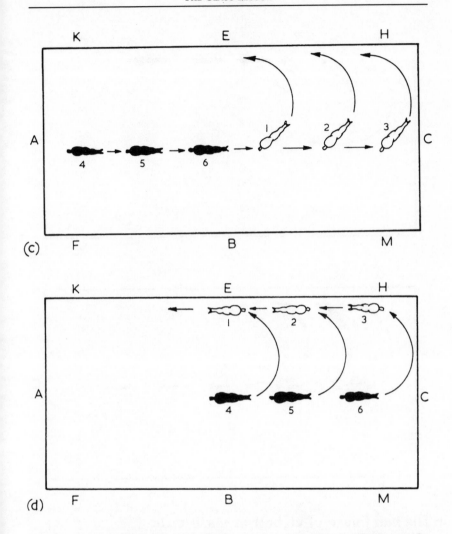

Fig 12 The two rides circling: (a) Number 1 ride – circle left; (b) Number 2 ride – circle left; (c) Number 1 ride – ride away; (d) Number 2 ride – ride away

'Number one ride away', whereupon each member of number one ride makes a half circle to the left back on to the track, so that they arrive back on the track in their original order. As the first rider in number two ride approaches G, the command is given, 'Number two ride away', and number two ride makes individual half circles to the left so that the riders arrive back on the track in their original order and the whole ride is back on the track on the left rein in correct order.

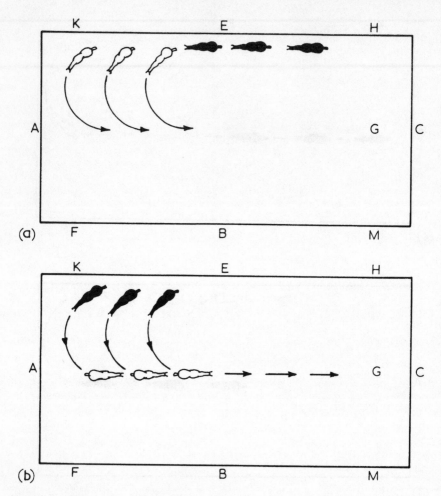

(a)

(b)

✳The half figure-of-eight (Figs 13a, b, c, d)

As the leading file reaches the K marker on the left rein, the command is given, 'Number one ride, half figure-of-eight'. Number one ride performs exactly the same exercise as in circling to the left, and continues in single file down the centre line towards C with rider number 3 leading. As the leading file of number two ride approaches the K marker, the command is given 'Number two ride, half figure-of-eight' and number two ride makes the same exercise circling left and continuing down the centre line, in single file towards C, in line with number one ride. As the leading rider (number 3) approaches G the command is given, 'Number one ride

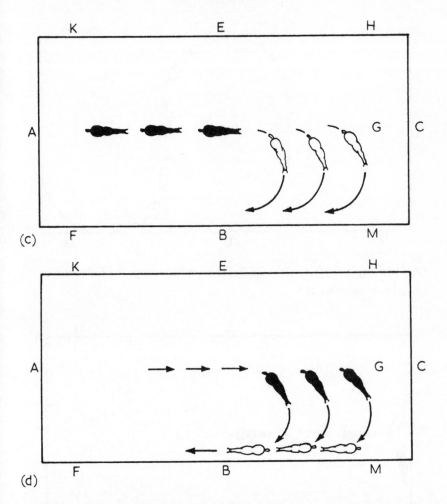

Fig 13 The two rides performing the half figure of eight: (a) Number 1 ride – half figure of eight; (b) Number 2 ride – half figure of eight; (c) Number 1 ride – ride away; (d) Number 2 ride – ride away

away'. Here number one ride makes individual half circles to the right back on to the track, with rider number 1 in leading file so changing the rein. As the leading rider in number two ride approaches G the command is given, 'Number two ride away' and number two ride makes individual half circles back on to the track to the right, so forming single file on the track with rider number 4 leading behind number one ride.

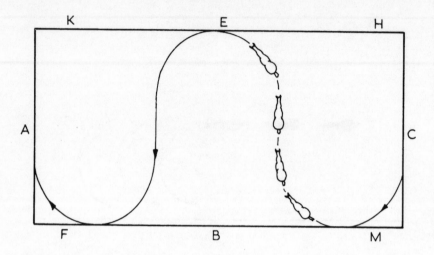

Fig 14 In single file from C, make three serpentine loops the full width of the school, finishing at A

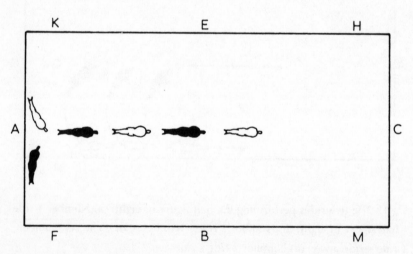

Fig 15 Forming a double ride – at A the odd numbers turn right and the even numbers turn left

The three-loop serpentine (Fig 14)

The command for this exercise should be given as the leading file passes E on the right rein: 'In single file from C, make three serpentine loops, the full width of the school, finishing at A.'

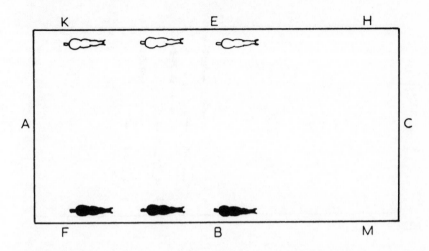

Fig 16 The ride on the right rein is responsible for the pace and the ride on the left rein is responsible for the dressing

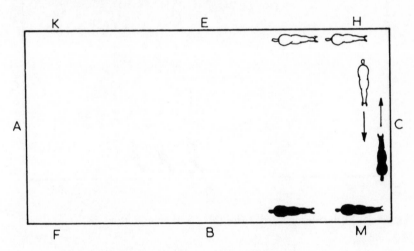

Fig 17 The two rides pass left hand to left hand at C

Forming a double ride (Figs 15, 16, 17)

The command is given on either rein as the leading file passes the E or B marker: 'The leading file turns down the centre at A (or C), and at C (or A), odd numbers pass to the right, even numbers to the left, and form a double ride.'

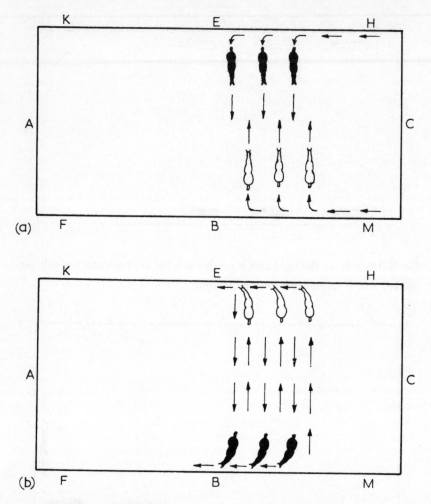

Fig 18 (a) Both rides inwards turn; (b) ...and change the rein

Most of the exercises that are made as a single ride can also be made as a double ride. This work is useful as it encourages the riders to ride with more precision and it increases their awareness of other riders. It also adds variation to the school work and is usually enjoyed by the class.

The ride on the right rein is responsible for the pace, and the ride on the left rein is responsible for the dressing.

When the two rides meet on the track, they pass left hand to left hand.

Figures 18–21 show a selection of useful exercises which can be used for a double ride.

These exercises can be made on the left or the right rein, but sufficient warning should be given by a cautionary word of

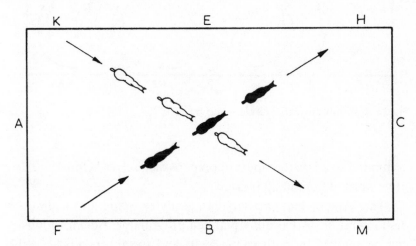

Fig 19 At F and K inwards incline and change the rein

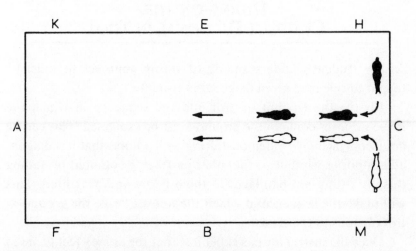

Fig 20 At C by half sections down the centre

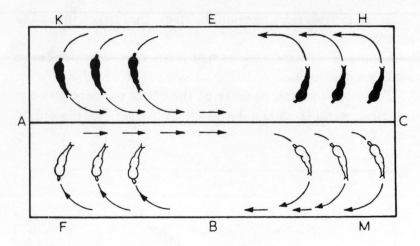

Fig 21 Both rides inwards circle – and away

command to allow the riders to prepare themselves before the executive word of command is given.

This type of class activity can easily be made into a show or demonstration. A carefully planned programme, ridden to music, can be enjoyed by both participants and spectators alike. As the class improves, work in canter and lateral work can be included.

RIDING ON THE CORRECT DIAGONAL IN TROT

As the student's understanding of riding improves he must be taught to ride on a given diagonal in rising trot.

Firstly, the rhythm of trot and the sequence in which the horse's hooves come to the ground must be explained. This can be done convincingly by demonstrating with a horse that has diagonally opposite white legs, the other pair being coloured or, failing this, by fitting red bandages to the off fore and near hind. This will make the sequence in which the hooves strike the ground in trot obvious to the class.

Once the instructor has explained that the horse's feet come to the ground in diagonally opposite pairs in two-time, it will be easy for the rider to understand that in rising trot he lifts his seat out of the saddle as one diagonal pair comes to the ground, and lowers it onto the saddle as the other diagonal pair comes to the ground, thereby producing the 'one-two' rhythm of rising trot.

To enable the rider to identify the diagonal on which he is riding, he should be made to count out loud the rhythm of the pace as he rides in rising trot. He should then change from counting 'one-two', to 'up-down', and next, should be told to look down at the horse's outside shoulder: as the shoulder comes back, he should lower his seat to the saddle. In this way he will lower his seat to the saddle as the outside foreleg and inside hindleg come to the ground together, and lift his seat out of the saddle as the inside foreleg and outside hindleg come to the ground.

He can be taught to identify the diagonal on which he is riding by looking down at the inside shoulder and lifting his seat out of the saddle as the inside shoulder comes back. This will achieve the same result, but is usually found to be less easy to pick up than lowering the seat to the saddle on the outside diagonal.

Once the student can successfully identify the diagonal on which he is riding, it is only a short step to being able to change it when necessary. This is best achieved by getting him to say 'up-down-up-down' in rhythm with the stride and to sit for two beats saying 'down-down' as he does so. When this is thoroughly mastered, the rider has made real progress along the road to understanding what is happening underneath him when he rides.

RIDING WITHOUT STIRRUPS

This work is one of the most important aspects of all the rider's training, developing confidence and playing a major part in establishing a deep, supple seat. It is best carried out in a dressage saddle to enable the rider to sit deep and to allow the leg to be long. The jumping or general purpose saddle is not entirely suitable for this training, as its seat tends to be longer and shallower, and the rider's leg, if allowed to be long, tends to come off the back of the saddle flap with the bottom of the flap catching on the top of the rider's boots. In fact it is best to remove the stirrups and leathers from the saddle altogether, but this is time-consuming and inconvenient. Even so, if the stirrup leathers are crossed over the saddle carelessly they will cause a lump of twisted leather under the rider's thigh and he will be uncomfortable; he may then sit on the back of the saddle to avoid the discomfort, which defeats the object of riding without stirrups. The stirrup-leather buckles should therefore be pulled down so that the leathers can be folded flat across the saddle, avoiding any uncomfortable bump under the rider's leg.

All the work normally done with stirrups can eventually be done without, although the instructor should remember the effect that too much sitting trot of a poor quality may have on his horses. The horses used for class instruction at this level will probably be hollow and unlikely to accept the rider's hand, and a great deal of novice sitting trot will tend to make them even more hollow.

Initially this work will be tiring for the rider, because he will probably tend to grip up and tense the muscles of the leg and upper body. He must be encouraged to relax and be at rest in the bottom of the saddle. Whilst as much of the inside of the rider's leg as possible must stay in contact with the saddle and the horse's side, he must not be allowed to grip, as this will tend to squeeze him up and out of the saddle.

To help the riders to sit deep in sitting trot they should be told to take both reins and the whip in the outside hand, and to hook one finger of the inside hand under the pommel of the saddle. In this way they can give themselves a pull down into the saddle and they are usually surprised at how much closer they can sit when doing this.

Rising trot without stirrups should not be taught to the novice rider as it tends to make him grip up and shorten his legs. It is, however, an excellent strengthening exercise for the competitive cross-country rider, point-to-pointer and polo player, and will be covered later in this book.

TEACHING THE AIDS

Teaching the correct way to apply the aids is perhaps the most difficult problem confronting the riding instructor. Most beginners start riding thinking that to make a horse go you kick him, to make him stop you pull on both reins, to turn right you pull the right rein and to turn left you pull the left rein. Unfortunately, where the beginner has had some experience on an untrained horse and perhaps under the guidance of an unskilled adviser, this is often the case.

However, the basic principles of the application of the aids must be clearly instilled in the student from the start. He must be taught to ride with a sure rein contact. It is desirable that one should ride with a light rein, but it is much more desirable that one should ride with a sure, steady, even but 'allowing' contact through the rein to the horse's mouth.

The rider should somehow be made to understand that the aids with the legs, seat and hands are private and confidential signals sent by the rider to the horse, and that they should hardly be visible to the spectator. When applying any aids the rider should have two fundamental requirements in mind: firstly, that he wants maximum response from the horse with minimum effort on the part of the rider, and secondly, that he should aim at one aid achieving one response.

It is very easy to teach the rider the effect of using the left rein or the right rein, or the left leg or the right leg; what is difficult is to teach him how much to use of each, and in what blend or combination. This is a question of feel, and is dependent upon the pupil's imagination and skill as a rider being carefully developed and guided by an expert instructor. Many pianists learn to read music and to strike the correct notes on the piano: few arrive on the concert platform because the majority have insufficient 'feel' to produce from the piano the full potential of the music. This theory very much applies to the riding of horses.

The basic theory of the classical application of the aids *must* be understood by the student, and is as follows:

**REIN OF INDIRECT OPPOSITION
IN FRONT OF WITHERS**
For sharp turn, while moving
or for turn on centre in place

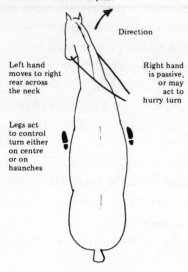

Direction

Left hand
moves to right
rear across
the neck

Right hand
is passive,
or may
act to
hurry turn

Legs act
to control
turn either
on centre
or on
haunches

REIN OF DIRECT OPPOSITION
For sharp turn, while moving
or turn on centre in place

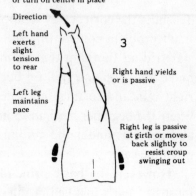

Direction

Left hand
exerts
slight
tension
to rear

3

Right hand yields
or is passive

Left leg
maintains
pace

Right leg is passive
at girth or moves
back slightly to
resist croup
swinging out

NECK REIN
For change of direction
without change of pace

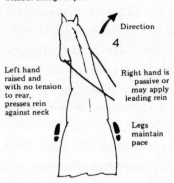

Direction

4

Left hand
raised and
with no tension
to rear,
presses rein
against neck

Right hand is
passive or
may apply
leading rein

Legs
maintain
pace

**REIN OF INDIRECT OPPOSITION
IN REAR OF WITHERS**
For right turn, while moving

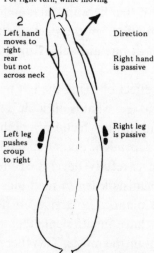

2

Left hand
moves to
right
rear
but not
across neck

Direction

Right hand
is passive

Left leg
pushes
croup
to right

Right leg
is passive

LEADING REIN
For turn on large curve

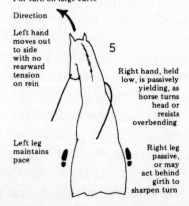

Direction

Left hand
moves out
to side
with no
rearward
tension
on rein

5

Right hand, held
low, is passively
yielding, as
horse turns
head or
resists
overbending

Left leg
maintains
pace

Right leg
passive,
or may
act behind
girth to
sharpen turn

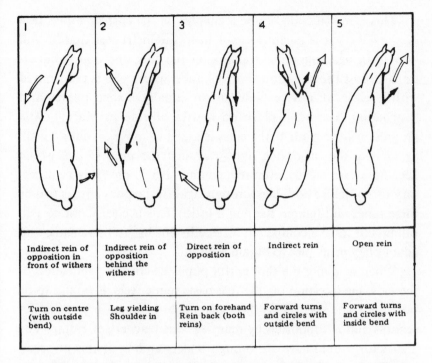

1	2	3	4	5
Indirect rein of opposition in front of withers	Indirect rein of opposition behind the withers	Direct rein of opposition	Indirect rein	Open rein
Turn on centre (with outside bend)	Leg yielding Shoulder in	Turn on forehand Rein back (both reins)	Forward turns and circles with outside bend	Forward turns and circles with inside bend

Fig 22 Two different schools of thought showing the five basic rein effects

a. The inside leg creates impulsion.

b. The outside leg controls the quarters and asks for canter.

c. The inside hand asks for the bend.

d. The outside hand receives the impulsion created by the inside leg and controls the impulsion, the speed and the bend in the neck.

The hand aids are made by a 'take-and-give' feeling with the fingers, as though the rider were squeezing a rubber ball in his hand. However, this aid will only have an effect with the correct rein contact.

The leg aids ask the horse to go forwards and are applied by closing the leg directly inwards, not by swinging the leg backwards and upwards as is often the seen. If the correct leg aid does not achieve the required response then it should *not* be increased, but must be repeated correctly and reinforced with the whip.

This is not intended to be a chapter on the correct application of the aids, but is meant to explain to the instructor that he will have to be versatile in his teaching of the aids, and make adaptations to suit the situation. For instance, where one is confronted with a class of novice children on equally novice ponies and instruction is to take place on a wild hillside in March, little progress will be made if the class is asked to move off into a walk by closing the inside leg lightly against the pony's side, whilst keeping a sure, steady, even rein contact. It will probably be necessary to say, 'close both legs strongly against the pony's sides two or three times and lighten the rein a little'. This is clearly not correct riding, but to be a competent instructor one has to be versatile and adapt one's principles to obtain a result.

When teaching the thoughtful pupil the correct application of the aids, the question of 'the five basic rein effects' is bound to be raised at some stage. This theory is taught in some very successful schools and is supported by many serious teachers of riding. The instructor should have a thorough understanding of this principle in order to be able to teach it or refute it, depending on his own convictions. Fig 22 shows how two leading authorities illustrate this principle. There is, however, a strong school of thought that the aids made with the reins are less complicated than this.

The complete rider will be able to apply the aids classically and correctly, and will be able to use legs, back, seat and hands strongly and effectively in an emergency, or where circumstances require it. The riding instructor must understand this, and should educate his students along these lines, being careful to note when they reach a stage of riding and horse-understanding at which they can absorb and appreciate this more sophisticated attitude towards the aids.

MOUNTED EXERCISES

These exercises are to improve the rider's confidence, suppleness, balance and co-ordination, and can be done at halt, walk, trot or canter both in a ride or on the lunge, and should be introduced to the student progressively through the paces. When they are carried out in a class lesson, and on the move, a reliable leading file is required who will not perform the exercises but will set a steady pace for the ride to follow.

Each rider should tie a knot in the reins so that they can be dropped on the horse's neck, and the whips should either be taken from the class by the instructor or be held by the rider between the thigh and the saddle. These exercises can be made with or without stirrups, and when made at trot are best made in sitting trot.

A selection of mounted exercises is shown in Fig 23.

a. Arm circling backwards: the rider raises both arms up above his head and circles them backwards in a rhythmical and relaxed manner. This improves suppleness and upper-body posture.

b. Alternate arm swinging: the arms are swung from front to rear alternately, thus improving suppleness.

c. Trunk twisting to the left and to the right: the arms are held out level with the shoulders, and the top part of the body is swung rhythmically from the left to right and right to left, twisting at the waist.

d. Right hand down towards right toe, or left hand down towards left toe. The arms are held out level with the shoulders, and the rider leans forward to touch the right toe with the right hand, or the left toe with the left hand. This improves suppleness and agility.

e. Right hand down towards left toe, or left hand down towards right toe. The instructions are the same as for the previous exercise, but the rider reaches across his horse's neck to touch the opposite toe.

f. Body swinging backwards and forwards: with the arms lightly folded, the rider swings the upper body forwards and backwards continuing to look ahead. The legs remain in the correct position.

Above all, suppleness and rhythm must be maintained, and the seat and leg kept in the correct position.

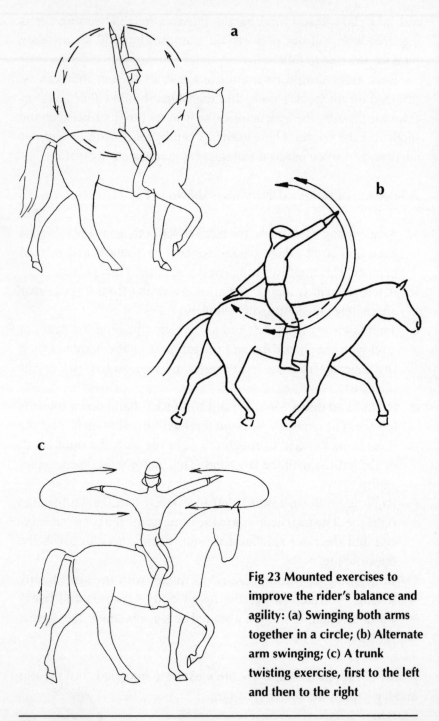

Fig 23 Mounted exercises to improve the rider's balance and agility: (a) Swinging both arms together in a circle; (b) Alternate arm swinging; (c) A trunk twisting exercise, first to the left and then to the right

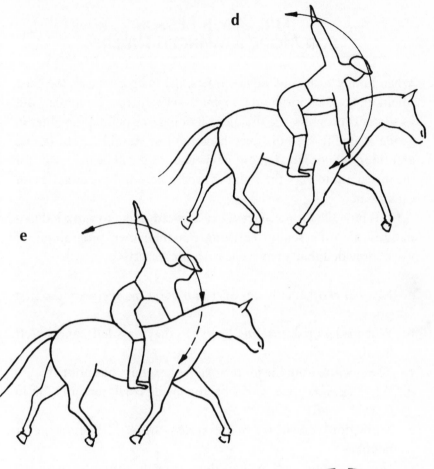

Fig 23 Mounted exercises to improve the rider's balance and agility: (d) Stretching the right hand down towards the right toe; (e) Stretching the right hand down towards the left toe; (f) Swinging the body both backwards and forwards

THE CLASS LESSON
FOR MORE ADVANCED RIDERS

When taking a class of novice riders, the instructor uses the class to obtain good control and maximum activity from each rider. But as students progress, the practice of riding one behind the other in a ride at one horse's distance becomes less suitable. Both horses and riders will progress at different rates, so it will be necessary for the instructor to vary the training programme and the exercises for each rider.

It is possible for up to eight experienced riders to work individually in a riding school carrying out their own programme of work, provided that a few basic rules are observed:

a. Normal gentlemanly conduct and good manners are the first priority.
b. When riders risk meeting head-on, they pass left hand to left hand.
c. The rider making the more advanced exercise has priority.
d. When in walk, one works on the inside track (about 1.5m in from the wall).
e. Transitions down are made across the A–C line whenever possible.
f. Conversations – other than those directly connected with the work in hand – are not permitted.
g. Riders who wish to halt to rest, do so across the A–C line.
h. No rider dismounts or leaves the school without the permission of the instructor.
i. Great care is taken in the use of the whip as punishment, in case other horses or riders are startled by such action.

In this way the instructor can set the programme of work for each pupil or group of pupils and give individual instructions as required.

In order to create a greater control and to give some variety to this work, it is sometimes helpful to divide the class into two

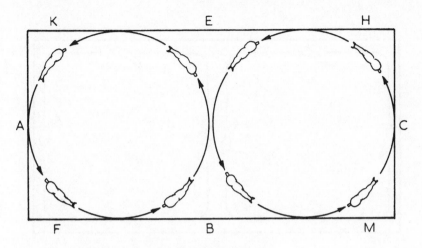

Fig 24 The divided class working on two circles

halves and work each half on a large circle, one half at A and the other half at C. The four riders in each ride space themselves out so that there is an equal distance between them (Fig 24). An important part of this exercise is that the riders should keep the correct distance between each other, not by making the circle smaller or by spoiling its shape by going further into the corner, but by maintaining the correct circle shape and lengthening or shortening the steps as necessary.

To help the riders to do this, 'circle points' should be marked on the wall to show each rider where he should 'brush' the track when making a true circle. This 'circle point' is midway between B or E and the corner of the school (Fig 25, p62); the circle can be changed to a square, or diamond, (Fig 26, p62) to encourage precise riding and to provide variety.

Transitions can be made up and down through halt, walk, trot, canter and rein-back as a class on the instructor's word of command. Work can include collected, working and medium paces (with the exception of medium canter): shoulder-in, travers, renvers, half-pirouettes and turns on the forehand can all be worked on under these circumstances.

Trotting poles can also be introduced into each circle in the

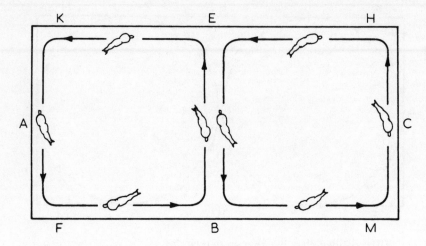

Fig 25 The divided class working in shoulder-in on two squares

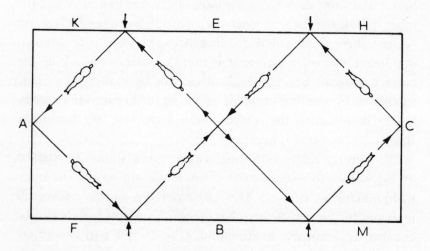

Fig 26 The divided class working on two diamonds

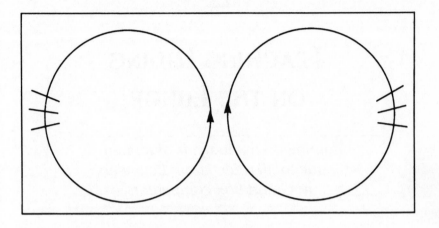

Fig 27 Trotting poles positioned on two circles

shape of a fan (Fig 27); these provide the opportunity to work on lengthening and shortening the steps in trot.

It is not necessary to have both rides working on the same rein; thus the ride at the A end of the school may be on the right rein, and the ride at the C end on the left. Changing the rein may be carried out in a variety of ways:

a. By turning down the centre line A to C or C to A, and then re-establishing the circle at the opposite end on the new rein.

b. By inclining across the long diagonal, passing left hand to left hand at X, and re-establishing the circle on the new rein at the opposite end of the school.

c. By a half-pirouette in walk.

d. By a turn on the forehand.

4

TEACHING RIDING
ON THE LUNGE

---

*Training on the lunge is of immense
value to all riders, from beginners
to Grand Prix competitors.*

For the beginner it is a good introduction to the horse, giving him confidence and helping him to develop his seat, and this was discussed in some detail in Chapter 2. For the improving rider it deepens his seat and hence improves his feel of correct paces, and most important of all, of well executed transitions. For the advanced rider it is a useful exercise for revision and correction; even the most talented and successful slip into bad habits, and need to return to school from time to time.

The basic principles of lungeing the horse for training the rider are the same at all levels. The horse must be correctly dressed and must be of a suitable temperament for the task. For the beginner rider it is sufficient that the horse should be safe, obedient and comfortable. Safety is a fundamental factor: the horse must not shy or take fright under any circumstances, but always remain placid and calm; a lunge horse that gives the beginner rider a fright by shying or running off will do very much more harm than good. It is not therefore necessary that this horse is an extravagant mover, and in fact it is better that he should walk and trot at a calm, steady pace, obedient to the instructor's command. Note that it is unlikely, although not impossible, that this horse will be able to work on the lunge at canter sufficiently slowly to be of value to the beginner.

The horse that is used for improving the advanced rider is a quite different animal. He must be capable of going correctly in walk, trot and canter, on the bit and in the correct outline. He must be capable of making good transitions both between and within the paces, and he must have good balance and impulsion.

When lungeing the more advanced rider on this horse, the side-reins are made a little shorter because the horse will be working in a more rounded outline, and the stirrups and leathers should be removed from the saddle altogether. However, if the rider can ride long enough without stirrups, but finds difficulty riding long enough *with* them, then they should be retained.

Although the beginner was introduced to rising trot on the lunge, this was for practical convenience only, and there is no place for this exercise for the competent rider. The main value of training on the lunge for the advanced rider is to correct and improve the seat and to blend the movement of his body into the movement of the horse through transitions and variations of pace.

The truly expert instructor will place great value on a good lunge horse; this helpmate is often a senior member of the stable who has proved himself capable of playing this very important role. He should not, however, be confined to a life of 15m circles on side-reins: an occasional hack in the country or an hour or two each day in the field will be sufficient to keep him fresh and rewarded.

To lunge any rider successfully, the instructor must be able to lunge his horse correctly, maintaining a suitable speed, rhythm and impulsion in each pace; in fact, his standard of lungeing must be exemplary. He must stand still in the centre of the circle to ensure that the circle is round, and must keep a sure contact through an untwisted rein, with the spare end looped tidily in his hand. The whip must be used carefully and correctly, towards the horse's hindquarters to increase the speed or impulsion and to send him forwards, or towards the shoulder to keep him out on the circle; under these circumstances it must never startle the horse or make him jump. Frequent changes of rein must be made to ensure equal development of both horse and rider. At the same time, the instructor must devote most of his attention to the rider, quickly

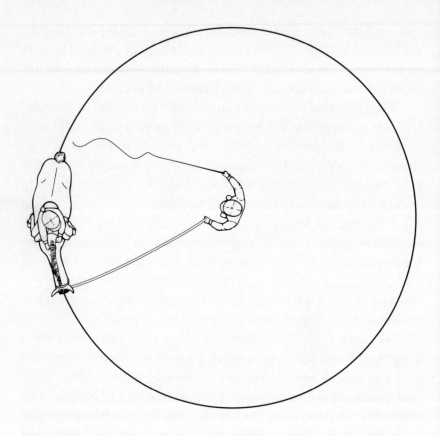

Fig 28 Lungeing, showing the relative position of the horse to the trainer and whip

identifying faults and problems and suggesting remedial exercises.

Twenty to thirty minutes on the lunge is sufficient time for any rider to achieve maximum benefit from this exercise. The observant instructor will identify the moment when the pupil is at his best, and this is the time to stop, as deterioration may follow. Whenever possible, all training should end on a good note.

5

TEACHING THE DRESSAGE RIDER

The complete riding instructor will understand that riders fall into two broad classes: those who wish to use the horse as a means of transport; and those who wish to train their horses for any branch of equitation, along classical lines and to the limits of the horse's physical and mental capabilities. Neither of these groups should be ignored or decried by the professional instructor.

The first group will want their horses to be willing and obedient, to start and stop when required, to turn left and right and jump. They may not be particular as to exactly how these ends are achieved, and will probably not be sufficiently skilled riders to obtain results without the use of various bits, martingales and other artificial aids. It is essential that the riding instructor understands the requirements of this branch of the riding fraternity and that he is an expert in the use of martingales, schooling martingales, draw-reins and running-reins and various types of popular bit.

Many of these riders are excellent horsemasters and stable managers who derive a great deal of enjoyment from their horses. They will often come to a riding instructor for help, and he must understand their attitude to riding and be able to assist them. On the other hand, there are those riders who wish to train their horses along classical lines without force or compulsion, but by the gradual and progressive development of the horse's physical and mental abilities. It is these riders and their horses that will be considered in this chapter.

Any horse can be trained as a dressage horse, but some are very much more rewarding than others because they possess a natural elegance, and also balance and quality of paces. Exactly the same applies to riders: they can all be trained as dressage riders, but some are much better suited than others because of their more favourable shape, elegance and temperament.

Probably the greatest problem that the instructor will face is training the novice rider who comes to him on an untrained horse. However, provided that the horse has not been spoiled previously, this combination can also be a most rewarding challenge. Under these circumstances three major courses of action must be followed:

a. The pupil must work on his own horse under instruction.
b. He must be trained on a well schooled horse from time to time so that he knows what he is aiming for.
c. The instructor must ride the pupil's horse to help put him on the right lines and to assess any difficulties that the horse may have and with which his pupil will have to cope.

The pupil must understand his ultimate aim clearly, and it should be reduced to as few words as possible. Once he realises that he is trying to put the horse in a position where he, the horse, can improve his own natural paces and outline, the pupil will be well on the way to understanding the true aim of dressage training. The Rules of the International Equestrian Federation state the following:

> The object of Dressage is the harmonious development of the physique and ability of the horse. As a result it makes the horse calm, supple, loose and flexible, but also confident, attentive and keen, thus achieving perfect understanding with his rider.
>
> These qualities are revealed by:
> the freedom and regularity of the paces;

the harmony, lightness and ease of the movements;
the lightness of the forehand and the engagement of the
hindquarters, originating in a lively impulsion;
the acceptance of the bridle, with submissiveness
throughout and without any tenseness or resistance.

The horse thus gives the impression of doing of his own
accord what is required of him. Confident and attentive,
he submits generously to the control of his rider, remaining
absolutely straight in any movement on a straight line and
bending accordingly when moving on curved lines.

His walk is regular, free and unconstrained. His trot is free,
supple, regular, sustained and active. His canter is united,
light and cadenced. His quarters are never inactive or
sluggish. They respond to the slightest indication of the
rider and thereby give life and spirit to all the rest of his
body.

By virtue of a lively impulsion and the suppleness of his
joints, free from the paralysing effects of resistance, the
horse obeys willingly and without hesitation and responds
to the various aids calmly and with precision, displaying a
natural and harmonious balance both physically and
mentally.

In all his work, even at the halt, the horse must be 'on the
bit'. A horse is said to be 'on the bit' when the hocks are
correctly placed, the neck is more or less raised and
arched according to the stage of training and the extension
or collection of the pace, and he accepts the bridle with a
light and soft contact and submissiveness throughout. The
head should remain in a steady position, as a rule slightly
in front of the vertical, with a supple poll as the highest
point of the neck, and no resistance should be offered to
the rider.

TEACHING THE PACES

Before the student of dressage attempts to have any effect on his horse he must understand the basic requirements of each of the horse's paces.

When teaching the timing and sequence of the paces, it is clearer if one refers to inside legs and outside legs rather than the left and right, or to the near and off. The inside legs are those on the concave side of the horse and the outside legs are those on the convex side. Consequently the inside legs are not necessarily those on the inside of the arena: for instance, a horse in counter canter will be bent away from the centre of the arena, and therefore if his inside legs are on his concave side they are on the outside of the arena.

The walk

There are four recognised types of walk: collected walk, medium walk, extended walk and free walk. The walk is a marching pace in which the footfalls follow one another in 'four-time'; they should be well marked and maintained in all work at the walk. The sequence of footfalls is outside hind, outside fore, inside hind, inside fore. When the four beats cease to be distinctly marked, even and regular, the walk is disunited or broken.

It is at the pace of walk that the imperfections of dressage are most evident, and this is also the reason why a horse should not be asked to walk 'on the bit' in the early stages of his training. Any attempt to increase collection before the horse is ready will spoil not only the collected walk, but the medium and the extended walk as well.

The trot

The trot should always be characterised by free, active and regular steps, and the horse should move into it without hesitation. It is a pace in two-time in which the feet come to the ground in diagonally opposite pairs, outside hind and inside fore together, followed by the inside hind and outside fore together. There is a period of suspension between each pair coming to the ground when in fact no feet are on the ground.

The quality of the trot is judged by the general impression given, the regularity and elasticity of the steps – originating from a supple back and well engaged hindquarters – and by the ability to maintain the same rhythm and natural balance.

The following trots are recognised: collected trot, working trot, medium trot and extended trot.

Collected trot The horse remains 'on the bit', and moves forwards with his neck raised and arched. The hocks, being well engaged, maintain an energetic impulsion, thus enabling the shoulders to move with greater ease in any direction. The horse's steps are shorter than in the other trots, but he is lighter and more mobile.

Working trot A pace between collected and medium trot, in which a horse, not yet trained and ready for collected movements, nevertheless shows himself to be properly balanced and, remaining 'on the bit', goes forwards with even, elastic steps and good hock action. The expression 'good hock action' does not mean that collection is a required quality of working trot; it only underlines the importance of an impulsion originating from the activity of the hindquarters.

Medium trot A pace between working and extended trot, but 'rounder' than the latter. The horse goes forwards with free and moderately extended steps and obvious impulsion from the hindquarters. The rider allows the horse, remaining 'on the bit', to carry his head a little more in front of the vertical than at the collected and the working trot, and allows him at the same time to lower his head and neck slightly. The steps should be as even as possible, and the whole movement balanced and unconstrained.

Extended trot The horse covers as much ground as possible. Maintaining the same tempo, he lengthens his steps to the utmost, an ability which results from great impulsion generated from the

a) at walk

b) at trot

c) at canter

**Figs 29 The sequence of
the horse's footfalls at
three different paces:**
a) at walk
b) at trot
c) at canter

hindquarters. The rider allows the horse, remaining 'on the bit', to lower and extend his neck in order to prevent his action from becoming higher. The fore feet should touch the ground on the spot towards which they are pointing.

The canter

Canter is a pace in three-time. The outside hindleg starts the pace, followed by the inside hind and outside forelegs together, followed by the inside foreleg, which is the leading leg. There is then a moment of suspension when there are no legs on the ground at all. The canter should be moved into without hesitation, with light, cadenced and regular strides.

The quality of the canter is judged by the general impression, and the regularity and lightness of the three-time pace – originating from the acceptance of the bridle with a supple poll and in the engagement of the hindquarters with an active hock action – and by the ability to maintain the same rhythm and a natural balance. The horse should remain straight on straight lines.

The following canters are recognised: collected canter, working canter, medium canter and extended canter.

Collected canter The horse remains 'on the bit', and moves forwards with his neck raised and arched. The collected canter is marked by the lightness of the forehand and the engagement of the hindquarters, ie is characterised by supple, free and mobile shoulders and very active quarters. The horse's strides are shorter than at the other canters, but he is lighter and more mobile.

Working canter A pace between the collected and the medium canter, in which a horse not yet trained and ready for collected movements shows himself properly balanced and, remaining 'on the bit', goes forwards with even, light and cadenced strides and good hock action. The expression 'good hock action' does not mean that collection is a required quality of working canter. It only underlines the importance of impulsion originated from the activity of the hindquarters.

Medium canter A pace between the working and the extended canter. The horse goes forwards with free, balanced and moderately extended strides and obvious impulsion from the hindquarters. The rider allows the horse, whilst he remains 'on the bit', to carry his head a little more in front of the vertical than at the collected and working canter, and allows him at the same time to lower his head and neck slightly. The strides should be long and as even as possible, and the whole movement balanced and unconstrained.

Extended canter The horse covers as much ground as possible. Maintaining the same tempo, he lengthens his stride to the utmost, without losing any of his calmness and lightness, as a result of great impulsion from the hindquarters. The rider allows the horse, whilst he remains 'on the bit', to lower and extend his head and neck with the tip of his nose pointing more or less forward.

The dressage rider must have regular lessons on a horse with good quality paces, so that he can constantly improve his recognition and understanding of the correct execution of the basic paces.

He must vary his work so that the horse is not always in the manège or indoor school. The instructor must ensure also that the horse is given a balanced programme of work, both in the riding school and out in the country to refresh him and give him some variation.

Once the dressage trainer has established in his pupil an understanding of the qualities that go to produce good basic walk, trot and canter paces, he must train him to make transitions within those paces: he must make collected, medium and extended walk; collected, working, medium and extended trot and canter; and finally piaffe and passage.

The trainer must explain these differences within each pace to avoid confusion. And whilst the more imaginative teacher will find various ways in which to explain ideas and concepts to his pupil, he must, once again, have a clear idea of the International Equestrian Federation's definitions.

THE DRESSAGE RIDER'S POSITION

The position of the dressage rider is of primary importance for three reasons: first of all, to give the horse a balanced load to carry, as a well balanced load is easier to carry than an unbalanced load; secondly, to enable him to be really effective by the correct application of the aids; and thirdly, to enable him to look as elegant as possible.

Ideally, the dressage rider should be slim and have good physical proportions. A long slender leg is an advantage, as is a slim body with a naturally elegant carriage. Overweight riders or those with short, fat limbs are not well suited to dressage riding.

By studying and analysing the seat and position of the dressage experts, the dressage instructor should develop a clear mental picture of the correct seat of the dressage rider. A clear idea of the correct seat will help him to obtain the best from his pupil, having taken into account any natural limitations resulting from a less-than-perfect conformation.

Throughout any movement the dressage rider must give an impression of easy elegance, and he must *never* show any signs of difficulty, frustration or exasperation. The dressage instructor must insist upon this attitude being maintained throughout training.

Choosing the right tack

To enable the dressage rider to sit in the correct position he must ride in the correct saddle. Money expended on a good dressage saddle which is a perfect fit for both horse and rider is a most rewarding investment (Fig 30). The reins are also an important part of the dressage rider's equipment, and should be narrow, leather ones. Rubber, plaited, nylon or webbing reins are unsuitable for dressage riding, as the feel in the fingers lacks subtlety.

ESTABLISHING THE HORSE'S OUTLINE

Before the lesson commences, and whilst the rider is adjusting his tack and mounting, the horse must be made to stand still on the

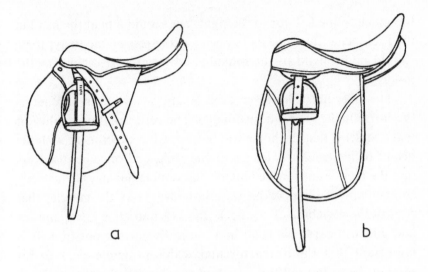

Fig 30 The different saddles used for jumping and dressage: (a) The jumping saddle; (b) The dressage saddle

centre line of the school at a correct halt, with all four feet square and with equal weight on each leg.

As in all riding training, the lesson must start with a warming-up period in which the horse is allowed to walk on a long rein with a low head carriage. He must, of course, comply with the basic rules in that he must go forwards, remaining straight and calm during this warming-up period.

After five minutes or so the rider should be told to take up the reins and correct his position, whereupon he takes up the rein contact that he intends to keep throughout his ride, except during periods of rest. The horse must therefore now work *on the bit*, and to achieve this the rider must give the horse an acceptable hand: that is, the horse should be allowed to go freely forwards and to adjust the height of his head and the length of his neck as he wishes. It must, however, be made clear to the pupil that the horse's head must *not* be pulled into position by the use of the hands; he must be allowed to adjust the height of his head and the length of his neck whilst given an acceptable hand, until the required relaxation is achieved. The rider must not allow him to bend his neck too much to the left nor to the right, but should aim at the bend in the neck being the same as the bend in the rest of the body; there should be no bend to the outside and no excessive bend to the inside.

The rider must, however, keep a sure, steady, even contact as the horse makes these adjustments. The result of this quality of rein contact is that the horse will be allowed to experiment with the height of his head and length of his neck, and once he discovers that the bit does not cause him any discomfort but stays in a steady contact with the bars of his mouth, he will relax the muscles that control the vertebrae of the neck, the axis and atlas joints and his jaw, and will carry his head in a naturally correct position. It is important that the instructor makes this principle clear to his student, because until this situation is achieved, the aids with the hands cannot be applied correctly.

Once the rider understands the principle of the rein contact and the horse is accepting his hand, he can encourage the horse to increase his impulsion by the use of the legs, reinforced if necessary by a long schooling whip.

In order that the horse can increase his impulsion he must bring his hindlegs further under him; this entails greater flexion of the hip, stifle and hock joints and consequently a lowering of the croup. The lowering of the croup results in a lightening of the fore-hand, and provided that the horse has been able to cope with the increase in impulsion and has remained forward, straight, calm and on the bit, considerable progress has been made towards establishing a correct outline. Where an increase in impulsion results in the horse losing any of the three basic qualities of being forward, straight and calm, or causes him to give up his acceptance of the rider's hand, then the increase in impulsion must be given up and the basic requirements re-established.

TEACHING FEEL

It is comparatively easy for the instructor to teach his pupil the principle of applying the aids with the legs, the seat and the hands.

The difficulty comes when trying to explain how much any particular aid should be applied. The rider has only a very few aids at his disposal with which to ask his horse to perform a wide range of activities, from standing still at halt, through walk, trot and canter, right up to piaffe and passage. In some cases the aids applied for two very different exercises appear to be identical: for instance, the aids for canter right and half-pass right. When asking the horse to canter right the rider bends the horse a little to the right, keeps the inside leg at the girth to ask for, or maintain impulsion, and draws the outside leg back to ask the horse to canter. When asking the horse to half-pass right he bends the horse a little to the right, keeps the inside leg at the girth to ask for or to maintain the impulsion, and draws the outside leg back to move his quarters to the right and so to make the half-pass. Thus the aids for these two movements are almost the same, the only difference being the way in which the outside leg is used. In the canter transition it is used as an executive command, 'canter *now*'. In half-pass it is used as a prolonged aid or a series of aids to ask the horse to move his quarters over. The use of these aids and their effectiveness depends on the rider's feel, and it is this feel which is difficult to teach.

One of the most useful exercises for improving the rider's 'feel' is to lengthen and shorten the steps. This can be done in walk, trot or canter, but is best started in trot where both speed and impulsion are more easily controlled. The steps are made shorter by maintaining the impulsion with the leg and decreasing the speed by the use of the outside hand. The correct blend of both leg and hand aids will result in the horse taking shorter steps but maintaining his balance, outline, forward movement and calmness; too much leg or hand will upset this balance. The ability to achieve this balance of the aids is the rider's 'feel'. To lengthen the steps the rider asks for an increase in impulsion with the leg, and allows the horse to take longer steps by lengthening his outline, stretching the head and neck forwards. To achieve long, elegant steps requires considerable 'feel' from the rider with regard to the blend of leg and hand aids necessary, the leg to increase the impulsion and the hand to control its build-up to result in good quality, long steps.

A rider will often find difficulty in maintaining the correct rein contact, and whilst it is most desirable that the rein contact should be light, it is much more important that it should be sure, steady and even. It is better that the rider should have a little more weight in his hand and maintain a sure, steady, even contact than that he should have a light rein with a contact that is continually varying.

The horse's 'stiff side' and 'soft side'

It is dangerous for the riding instructor to make generalisations, but it is fairly safe to say that all horses are more stiff on one rein than the other. Usually a horse is more stiff on the right than on the left, and many reasons have been put forward for this. None of them is convincing, however, other than that horses are left- or right-handed, rather like human beings, and that few of us are truly ambidextrous. The fact that a horse is more stiff to the right than to the left does not mean that he will find all his work on the right rein more difficult; in fact there are some exercises that he may well find easier to the right than to the left – shoulder-in is one of these.

From the riding instructor's point of view it is important to identify as soon as possible on which rein the horse is stiff, and to know how to plan his work to cope with this difficulty. A horse is usually more stiff in one direction than the other, due to physical reasons which make his work in that direction difficult. It is therefore quite wrong to make him work predominantly on his stiff side until he becomes supple. No, the good trainer will start work on the rein on which the horse finds work easier, and as the work improves on that rein he will introduce a little work on the stiff side – but before the quality of the work deteriorates, or the horse starts to resist, he will change back to the easier rein. As the horse improves on the soft side, so he will improve on the stiff side, and it is wrong to work him on his stiff side for long periods in the hope that his suppleness will improve.

TEACHING THE RIDER TO USE THE DOUBLE BRIDLE

The dressage rules require that for dressage tests, horses should be bitted as follows:

Preliminary and Novice standard: ordinary snaffle.

Elementary standard: ordinary snaffle or simple double bridle, as specified on the test sheet.

Medium standard: ordinary snaffle or simple double bridle, as specified on the test sheet.

Advanced standard: simple double bridle.

So as soon as the rider can ride his horse freely forward in a snaffle with a constant correct outline, and on the bit both when going straight forward and in lateral movements, he may be introduced to the double bridle.

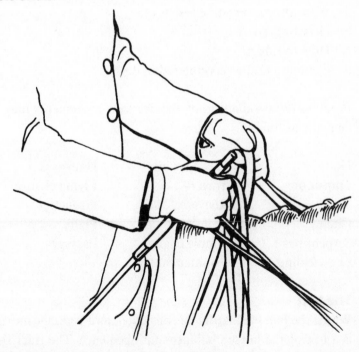

Fig 31 The reins of the double bridle correctly held

At first the rider should be taught the basic way in which to hold four reins, with the curb rein round the third finger of each hand and the bridoon rein round the little finger of each hand. The curb chain should be a link or two longer than normal at first, and whilst the rider is mastering the art of holding four reins there should be little or no contact on the curb rein. As he progresses, the curb rein contact can be taken up and the curb chain correctly adjusted. He must be trained to take up the curb rein and let it out smoothly as required.

THE DRESSAGE MOVEMENTS

The riding instructor, having established in his pupil a clear understanding of the requirements of the basic paces at walk, trot and canter, must introduce him progressively to the dressage movements. This work can conveniently be divided into four aspects:

a.   What the movement consists of.
b.   How to prepare for it.
c.   How to ride it.
d.   Common faults encountered in it.

Progressive introduction of the dressage movements may usefully be made as follows:

Halt	Shoulder-in	Half-pass
Transitions	Travers	Flying change
Turns	Renvers	Pirouettes
Circles	Rein-back	Piaffe
Serpentines	Simple change	Passage
Leg-yielding	Counter canter	

The halt
Whilst the halt can hardly be considered as a dressage movement, it is a test of the horse's balance and obedience. The rider should be taught the correct aids to ask the horse to come to halt and it must

be emphasised that a good halt can only come from a well balanced walk, trot or canter. It is unlikely that the horse will halt correctly if the pace from which he is making the halt is unbalanced or of poor quality.

The practice of halting incorrectly and then tapping the horse's legs with the stick to adjust those that are left behind should be discouraged as it is approaching the problem from the wrong end. A good halt will only come from a good quality preceding pace and correct application of the aids.

Transitions

The International Equestrian Federation Rules demand that:

> The changes of pace and speed should be clearly shown at the prescribed marker; they should be quickly made, yet must be smooth and not abrupt. The rhythm of a pace should be maintained up to the moment when the pace is changed or the horse halts. The horse should remain light in hand, calm and maintain a correct position.
>
> The same applies to transitions from one movement to another, for instance, from the passage to the piaffe and vice-versa.

However, a good transition is the joining together of two good quality paces. As both horse and rider improve in the execution of correct basic paces, so the transitions will improve: in teaching the rider to make transitions correctly, he must learn that preparation is important, and that when making a change of pace, the first steps of the new pace can only be as good in quality as the last steps of the old pace. For instance, when making the transition from trot to walk the horse should go from a full pace in two-time trot to a full pace in four-time walk; if the quality of the trot is lacking impulsion or unbalanced, then the ensuing walk will be poor.

Downward transitions are usually more difficult to make correctly than upward transitions, and it will often be helpful to make them on a circle or at a corner rather than on a straight line.

The aids for each transition must be taught to, and clearly understood by the rider; but having achieved this, he must learn that the final result will depend on the way in which he applies those aids on any particular horse. Whilst the aids for any transition can be easily understood by most riders, it is the blend of leg, seat and hand aids that achieves a smooth, balanced transition. Any aid, or combination of aids, may be used as and when they are required. However, the rider's aim must be to achieve maximum response from the horse from minimum effort on his part; which means that the aids must, eventually, be reduced to the minimum.

Turns

When the horse makes a turn the dressage rules (as in the *Official Dressage Rule Book 1996*) demand that:

> He should adjust the bend of his body to the curvature of the line he follows, remaining supple and following the indications of the rider, without any resistance or change of pace, rhythm or speed.
>
> When changing direction at right angles, for instance when riding corners, the horse should describe one quarter of a circle of approximately 6m diameter at collected and working paces, and at medium and extended paces one quarter of a circle of approximately 10m diameter.

Circles

Making circles at walk, trot and canter is a basic requirement of dressage tests from Preliminary level upwards.

The circle should have no corners and no flat sides. The horse must be bent throughout his entire length on the circumference of the circle. It is clear, therefore, that the novice horse will only be asked to make large circles, and only as his work progresses and he becomes more advanced, will the circles that he is asked to make become smaller. This is because a high degree of suppleness and agility is required for a horse to be able to make a circle of 15m or less without losing his outline, tempo, impulsion or the quality of the pace.

Serpentines

Serpentines are demanded in dressage tests in trot and canter, with more loops and therefore an increasing degree of difficulty as the tests become more advanced. They are a test of the horse's suppleness and his ability to make flowing, continual changes of direction, changing the bend and at the same time maintaining his balance and correctness of pace.

The work should start in trot and can later be made in canter. When making serpentines in trot the important point is to change the bend in the horse smoothly to conform with the curve of the serpentine track. The rider must apply the aids in good time to avoid upsetting the balance of the horse or interfering with his rhythm and free, forward movement. To help the horse change the bend as he changes direction, the serpentine loops should be made somewhat pear-shaped to start with, and less pear-shaped as the work improves.

Work on the serpentine should be started by making quite small loops off the track, a little over a meter in length, taking great care to ensure that the bend of the horse stays correct throughout the movement. These loops should be increased until they are made the full 20m width of a dressage arena.

Unless otherwise stated, serpentines in canter will include at least one loop in counter canter, so these cannot be attempted until the canter is short and light enough to perform counter canter correctly and without loss of balance. The same principles of rhythm and free, forward movement apply to serpentines in canter as they do in trot, *but* in canter the bend in the horse must be maintained towards the leading leg throughout the serpentine loops.

The work in canter should also be started by making small loops off the long side of the school, but the trainer must take care that the hind feet follow in the line of the tracks made by the fore feet, and that the horse does not move on two tracks, making half-pass off the track and leg-yielding back on to the track.

Leg-yielding

In this movement the horse should be quite straight except for a slight bend at the poll, so that the rider is just able to see the superciliary arch and nostril on the inside. The inside legs pass and cross in front of the outside legs; the horse looks away from the direction in which he is moving.

Leg-yielding on the diagonal The horse is quite straight except for a slight bend at the poll, so that the rider is just able to see his superciliary arch and nostril; the horse looks away from the direction in which he is moving (Fig 32).

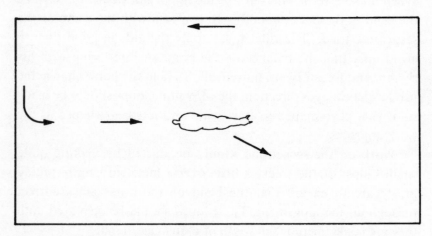

Fig 32 Leg-yielding on the diagonal

Fig 33 Leg-yielding along the wall

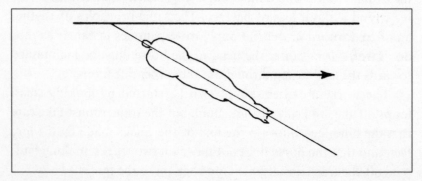

Leg-yielding along the wall See the description of leg-yielding on the diagonal, and Fig 33.

Leg-yielding is a controversial exercise totally shunned by some trainers but used extensively and with good effect by others. Its advantages and disadvantages should be studied by the riding teacher so he forms his own principles along firm, well considered lines.

Those who support leg-yielding do so for the following reasons:

a. As an introductory exercise to sideways and forward movement, it is an easy one for the horse to execute.
b. No degree of collection is required, so it can be started in working paces earlier than shoulder-in.
c. It has a good suppling effect on the horse.

Those who do not support it are of the opinion that:

a. It is an unattractive exercise which is not included in the classical repertoire.
b. The bend in the horse is opposite to the direction in which is moving.
c. To bend the horse at the poll only, may cause him to tilt his head to the left or to the right.
d. It invariably causes problems when the horse is asked to perform half-pass, because it may encourage the horse to lead with the quarters and to have insufficient bend.

When teaching leg-yielding, the instructor must guard against two major faults: firstly, he must ensure that the horse is kept quite straight, the only bend being at the poll; and secondly, the rider's leg that is asking the horse to yield should not be drawn back behind the girth, as this may cause the quarters to lead the movement.

Shoulder-in

The *Official Dressage Rule Book 1996* describes shoulder-in thus:

> The horse is slightly bent round the inside leg of the rider. The horse's inside foreleg passes and crosses in front of the outside leg; the inside leg is placed in front of the outside leg. The horse is looking away from the direction in which he is moving.
>
> Shoulder-in, if performed in the right way, with the horse slightly bent round the inside leg of the rider, and at the correct angle, is not only a suppling movement but also a collecting movement, because the horse at every step must move his inside hindleg underneath his body and place it in front of the outside, which he is unable to do without lowering his inside hip.

Shoulder-in is performed 'along the wall' at an angle of about 30 degrees to the direction in which the horse is moving.

This exercise is one of the riding instructor's closest allies. It has a most profound effect on the horse's suppleness; it helps very much in improving collection; it is the correct and most effective introduction to lateral work; it improves the canter strike-off; helps to straighten the crooked horse; and when performed correctly is a graceful and elegant movement to watch. Few movements in equitation can boast such a list of beneficial effects on the horse.

There are, however, varying views on how this exercise should be performed, and once again the riding instructor must have a clear knowledge of each version before he can confidently proceed with teaching shoulder-in.

The first school of thought is that the horse should form an angle to the track of about 30 degrees with his hips at an angle to the wall and both fore and hind inside legs crossing over the outside legs. The horse has some consistent bend throughout the length of his body. This is shown quite clearly in the illustration to the dressage rules (Fig 34). When shoulder-in is done in this way there is a tendency for it to be more like leg-yielding, particularly if the bend is insufficient or the pace lacks collection.

Fig 34 The shoulder-in at an angle of 30° with little bend

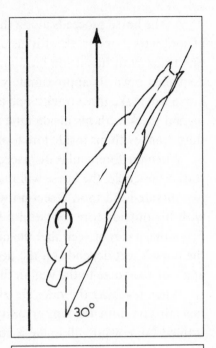

The alternative view of shoulder-in is that the horse's hips should remain at right-angles to the wall and that the hind feet should continue straight up the track without crossing or, in fact, making any deviation. The forehand only is taken in and the inside foreleg steps across the outside foreleg. This version requires greater suppleness and bend in the horse and a higher degree of collection, and is shown in Fig 35.

When explaining shoulder-in, the instructor will have to make clear to his pupil what is meant by two, three or four tracks. It is not possible for the rider to see how many tracks he is making as he rides, but he must know the meaning of these expressions so that he can understand the work more clearly and be able to comply with the instructor's wishes.

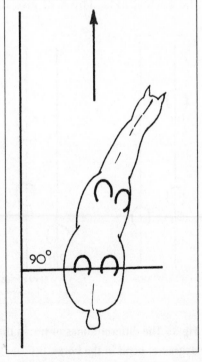

Fig 35 The shoulder-in with the hips positioned at right-angles to the track, and bend for a 15m circle

As the horse proceeds along the straight line he makes two lines of footmarks: one track with his outside hind and outside fore, and one track with his inside hind and inside fore. If the forehand is displaced inwards approximately enough to start a 10m circle, a horse will make three tracks: one track with his outside hind foot, a second track with his inside hind foot and outside fore foot and a third track with his inside fore foot.

When the forehand is displaced still further to the inside as if to start a 6m circle, the horse will make four lines of tracks: one with his outside hind foot, a second with his inside hind foot, a third with his outside fore foot and a fourth with his inside fore foot. From this it can be seen that the number of lines of tracks made by the horse's feet depends on the degree of bend in the horse, or the angle of the horse to the wall in the unbent horse (Fig 36).

When teaching the rider shoulder-in, it is again a great advantage to give him the opportunity to perform the exercise on a trained horse who will make a correct shoulder-in in response to the correct aids. This will give the rider a feel of the blend of the

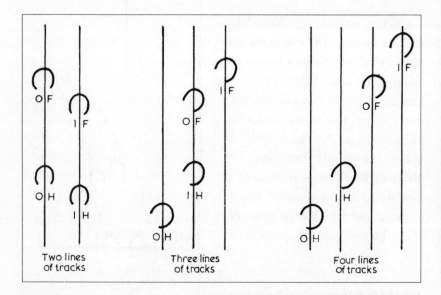

Fig 36 The different lines of tracks that can be made, depending on the degree of bend in the horse

aids required to achieve the exercise. Where this is not possible it is a case of 'the blind leading the blind' – although in practical every-day circumstances this is a typical situation with which the riding instructor must learn to cope.

Once the pupil fully understands what is required of his horse, he must consider carefully the aids that he will use to perform this movement, and must go through them in his mind before he attempts to put them into practice on his horse.

A convenient and effective way to introduce this exercise to both horse and rider is to start in walk by making a circle from the half marker on the right rein. Let us say that we plan to make the circle from E. The size of the circle will depend on the degree of training of the horse: it must be as small as he can manage without losing his balance, rhythm, outline, or his acceptance of the rider's hand; thus for the novice horse it may be 15–18m, for the more advanced horse 10–12m, and for the advanced horse a volte of 6m.

As the rider completes the circle he continues as though he is going to make a second circle, but just as the horse has taken one step off the track with the forehand and his hips have arrived at the E marker, the rider uses the fingers of his outside hand to say 'No – do not go any further forward on the circle', and he may use the outside hand with a slight opening effect to guide the horse along the track. The inside hand maintains the bend to the right, the inside leg is used at the girth to maintain the impulsion, and the outside leg remains in contact ready to prevent the quarters from swinging out. The rider's hips remain parallel to the horse's hips and his shoulders are turned in a little so that they remain parallel to the horse's shoulders. Equal distribution of weight is maintained on each seat-bone.

If three or four good steps in shoulder-in are obtained the horse should be sent energetically forwards, not by taking the fore-hand back on to the track, but by going forwards on the circle made by the bend of the shoulder-in. Once satisfactory progress has been made in walk and four to five good quality steps can be made in shoulder-in on both reins, then the exercise can be attempted in trot.

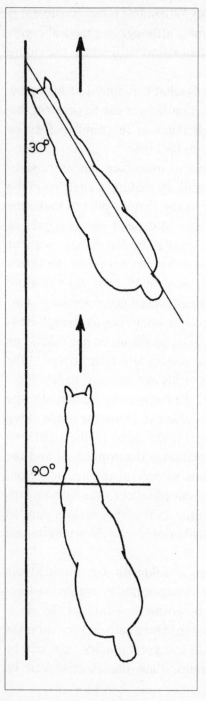

Fig 37 The travers with the shoulders at an angle of 30° to the line of progress

Work on this exercise is started in walk as both horse and rider have more time to organise their thoughts and actions. However, once they have both begun to understand what is required at walk, they should progress to trot, as at trot most horses find the production and maintenance of impulsion easier than at walk. Shoulder-in must be made with impulsion if it is to play its full part in the further training of horse and rider; performed correctly, it is invaluable.

Travers

In travers, according to the dressage rules the horse should be slightly bent round the inside leg of the rider. The horse's outside legs pass and cross in front of the inside legs; the horse is looking in the direction

Fig 38 The travers with the shoulder at an angle of 90° to the line of progress and the hindquarters taken in

in which he is moving. The exercise is performed 'along the wall' or, preferably, on the centre line, at an angle of about 30 degrees to the direction in which the horse is moving (Fig 37).

Travers is an exercise very much akin to half-pass. Shoulder-in requires that the forehand is displaced inwards with the front legs crossing over and the quarters remaining square on the track (or nearly so, depending on the horse's development and on the school of thought to which the rider subscribes). Travers requires that the hindquarters are displaced inwards and that the forehand stays straight on the track, the hindlegs crossing over and the forelegs continuing to go straight (Fig 38). The same difference of opinion exists regarding this exercise as in shoulder-in: whether or not the horse should be bent to such a degree that either the hindquarters in shoulder-in, or the forehand in travers, should be straight on the track with the legs not crossing over, or whether they should be inclined inwards a little, the legs being required to cross over. It will be seen from the definition in the dressage rules that the latter is required. The aids to make travers, to comply with either school of thought, are similar and only a question of degree will differentiate between the two.

Travers can be started by asking the pupil to make shoulder-in along the wall, and on arriving at the half marker to circle inwards on a circle commensurate with the bend in the horse. As the horse's shoulders arrive back at the half marker and his head is pointing straight down the track, or nearly so, the rider draws the outside leg back behind the girth to ask the hindquarters to move sideways along the inner track, so causing the hindlegs to cross over. The inside leg remains at the girth to maintain the impulsion. The inside hand keeps the bend and asks for the direction, whilst the outside hand keeps a contact ready to prevent too great a bend in the neck or an increase in speed. Having completed the required number of steps in travers the rider must, with his inside leg, return the horse's hindquarters to the track to let him know that the hindquarters may only be displaced to the left or to the right on the clear instruction of the rider.

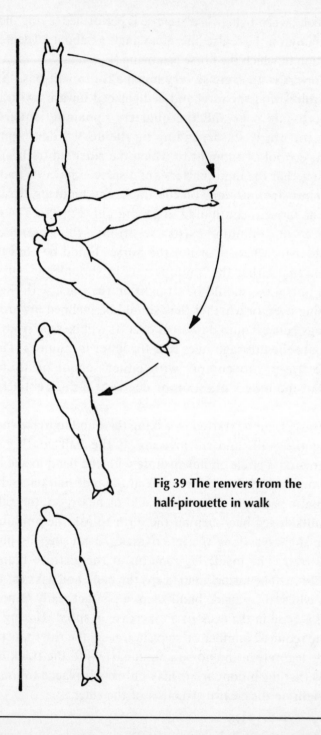

Fig 39 The renvers from the
half-pirouette in walk

Renvers

This is exactly the same exercise as travers, except that in renvers the forehand is brought in from the track, the horse still looking in the direction in which he is moving. Like travers, it is a suppling and obedience-improving exercise, but it is slightly more advanced in that the forehand, being off the track and without the guidance of the wall, may be more difficult to control.

When teaching this movement the easiest approach is from the half-pirouette in walk (Fig 39). The outside leg creates the position, the inside leg maintains the impulsion and helps maintain the bend, which is asked for with the inside hand. The outside hand controls the bend and the speed.

On completion of the renvers the forehand must be taken back onto the track and the horse ridden forwards with impulsion.

The rein-back

The following definition of the rein-back is taken from the dressage rules; the somewhat literal explanation in square brackets is my own.

1.   The rein-back is an equilateral, retrograde movement in which the feet are raised and set down almost simultaneously by diagonal pairs [each forefoot being raised and set down an instant before the diagonal hindfoot, so that, on hard ground, as a rule four separate beats are clearly audible]. The feet should be well raised and the hind feet remain well in line.

2.   At the preceding halt, as well as during the rein-back, the horse, although standing motionless and moving backwards respectively, remains 'on the bit', maintaining his desire to move forwards.

3.   Anticipation or precipitation of the movement, resistance to or evasion of the hand, deviation of the

quarters from the straight line, spreading or inactive hindlegs and dragging forefeet are serious faults.

4.   If in a dressage test a trot or canter is required after a rein-back, the horse should move off immediately into this pace, without a halt or an intermediate step.

For rein-back to comply with the demands of the dressage rules, a supple, well balanced and obedient horse is required. The stepping backwards that one sees out hunting or on the polo ground is for practical purposes only and is usually not 'rein-back'. Under these circumstances the horse is asked to step backwards by the rider's hand and he probably does not step back in two-time or straight; he probably also halts, having finished stepping back. All these actions would constitute serious faults in the rein-back when performed in a dressage test.

From the very start the instructor must instil in his pupil that rein-back is not made by pulling on the reins, but from a square, well balanced halt with the horse on the bit showing no signs of resistance. The rider is asked to close his legs against the horse's sides as if he were about to walk forward, but instead of allowing the horse to do so, he closes his fingers in a 'non-allowing' way which encourages it to step backwards. He must only step back the predetermined number of steps, and must then immediately step forwards, at whatever pace has been decided, without halting.

Where difficulty is experienced with this exercise the trainer can assist by tapping the horse lightly on the knee or fore-arm with the whip as the rider applies the aids. Above all the rider must not be allowed to pull.

Simple change of leg at canter

This is a change of leg where the horse is brought back into walk and, after two or at the most three steps, is re-started into canter with the other leg leading. It is yet another useful exercise for both the trainee horse and rider. For the horse it helps to improve his balance, his responsiveness to the aids and consequently his obedience. For the rider it helps to develop the subtle application of the aids and is a good exercise for establishing, in the rider's mind, the importance of the correct blend of seat, leg and hand in downward transitions. The simple change is best made across the diagonal of the school from a short, light canter with the rider asking the horse to walk at X, and having made three or four steps in walk, to strike off in canter on the new leading leg whilst still on the diagonal line.

In the downward transition the trainer must insist that the minimum amount of hand is used. The rider should sink softly down into the saddle, maintaining contact with the legs and using the fingers of the outside hand to apply a 'give-and-take' aid on the rein. It is important that the leg contact should be maintained to keep impulsion in the few steps in walk, otherwise the strike-off into the new canter will be difficult and incorrect.

The aids for walk to canter are the same as those used for trot to canter. The novice rider will often feel that he has to make stronger aids or use greater effort from walk to canter than from trot to canter. This is not so, and should not be necessary if the quality of the walk is sufficiently good for the horse to strike off into canter with ease.

Counter canter

This is a movement when the rider, on a circle to the left, deliberately makes his horse canter with the right canter lead (with the off-fore leading). The counter canter is a suppling movement. The horse maintains his natural flexion at the poll to the outside of the circle, and is therefore bent to the side of the leading leg. His conformation does not permit his spine to be bent to the line of the circle. The rider should especially endeavour to limit the deviation of the quarters to the outside of the circle, and restrict his demands according to the degree of suppleness of the horse. This is a particularly good suppling exercise for the horse and helps to develop his obedience, and for the rider it is a good lesson in 'feel'. Counter canter can be made in working canter on large circles and bends. The circle can only be made smaller as the canter becomes more collected. Counter canter is of no value if the horse is sloppy or off the bit.

Ideally the rider should ride in counter canter exactly as he would in canter, but in fact it may be necessary, on some horses, to maintain the correct bend by the use of the inside hand and leg, and to carry the outside leg a little behind the girth almost towards the canter aid.

The trainer must take care that the quarters are not allowed to swing either in or out on the circle. The counter-canter lesson can be started by making small loops off the long side of the school and returning to the track, taking care to maintain the correct bend in the horse. When making this preparatory work there is a danger that the hind feet will not follow in the line of the tracks made by the fore feet and that the horse will make a sort of half-pass off the track and leg-yield back onto the track.

These loops can be made deeper until the horse can be ridden from quarter marker to quarter marker, remaining in balanced counter canter through the corner and round the end of the school.

Half-pass

This is described in the rules of the International Equestrian Federation as follows:

> Half-pass. This is a variation of travers, executed 'on the diagonal' instead of 'along the wall'. The horse should be slightly bent round the inside leg of the rider in order to give more freedom and mobility to the shoulders, thus adding ease and grace to the movement, although the forehand should be slightly in advance of the quarters. [He should be as close as possible parallel to the long sides of the arena, although the forehand should be *slightly* in advance of the quarters.] The outside legs pass and cross in front of the inside legs. The horse is looking in the direction in which he is moving. He should maintain the same cadence and balance throughout the whole movement.

In order to give more freedom and mobility to the shoulders, which adds to the ease and grace of the movement, it is of great importance, not only that the horse is correctly bent and thereby prevented from protruding his inside shoulder, but also to maintain the impulsion, especially the engagement of the inside hind leg.

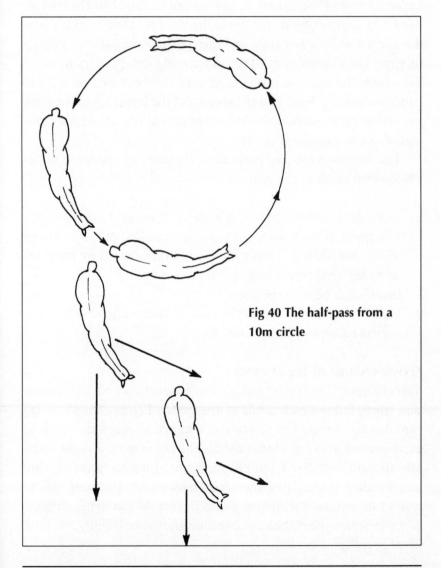

Fig 40 The half-pass from a 10m circle

If the preparatory work has been diligently carried out, and the horse is supple, responsive to the aids and capable of working with a degree of collection, the half-pass should come fluently and correctly. If, however, the preparatory work has been incorrect, various difficulties may be encountered, such as: the quarters leading; insufficient or incorrect bend; insufficient collection; and a lack of impulsion.

A successful way to start this work is to make a 10m circle in collected trot in the corner of the school to establish the correct bend. On completion of the circle the rider is asked to ride down the centre line for a few steps and then to draw back the outside leg to apply the quarter controlling aid, asking the quarters to move away from the leg. The inside hand asks for the bend, the outside hand controls the bend and the speed and the inside leg at the girth maintains the impulsion which is so important for the correct execution of this exercise (Fig 40).

The trainer must pay particular attention to the basic faults which often occur in this exercise:

a. The rider is unbalanced, with his weight usually to the outside.
b. The quarters lead, sometimes due to excessive or incorrect use of the outside leg. This is also sometimes caused by the rider using leg-yielding exercises in the same way.
c. Insufficient bend in the horse.
d. Loss of impulsion due to the rider neglecting to maintain the correct control with the inside leg.

Flying change of leg at canter

This change of leg is executed in close connection with the suspension which follows each stride of the canter. Flying changes of leg can also be executed in series, for instance at every stride, or at every second, third or fourth stride. The horse remains light, calm and straight with lively impulsion, maintaining the same rhythm and balance throughout the series concerned. In order not to restrict or restrain the lightness and fluency of the flying changes of leg in series, the degree of collection should be slightly less than usual at collected canter.

The flying change is probably the most exciting and satisfying exercise in equitation; it demands immense dexterity and understanding from the horse, and great feel and co-ordination from the rider. Before any rider is encouraged to teach his horse the flying change he must have had some training in this exercise on a horse that makes correct changes in response to correct aids. This is essential if the rider is to have any good effect on his own untrained horse.

There are a number of ways in which both horse and rider can be introduced to making the flying change, and it is recommended that the instructor should thoroughly understand, and be practised in each method. Whilst he may find one which is generally more advantageous, occasions will arise where one of the other methods may suit a particular horse or rider. A complete understanding of the various methods with their advantages and disadvantages will put the instructor in a much stronger position to defend the one which he chooses to use.

Before flying change is attempted, the trainer must ensure that the horse which his pupil is riding is capable of making the walk-to-canter and canter-to-walk transitions with balance and calmness. He must be able to perform these on both reins in the corners, going straight on the track and down the centre line. He must also be able to strike off in counter canter from walk on the track, going straight down the centre line and in the corners. Both rider and horse have a fair chance of achieving flying changes providing they are capable of these transitions, and the canter itself must have a degree of collection and be light and calm.

Flying change can be taught in three ways: 1. by changing the rein in canter from quarter marker to quarter marker and making the change from counter canter to true canter in the next corner; 2. it can be made from a half circle in canter off the track and by making the change as the track is met on the new rein; or 3. it can be made from counter canter on the large circle.

The first method By changing the rein in canter across the diagonal; it should be executed as follows: the lesson should, as always, start with ten or fifteen minutes of warming up exercise for both horse and rider. After this initial period, and whilst the horse is still fresh, the student should work on canter-to-walk and walk-to-canter transitions, starting in the corner and then straight on the track, followed by transitions down the centre line. Once these are established at a satisfactory standard, walk-to-counter-canter transitions can be practised, starting straight down the centre line, followed by straight on the track and finally in the corners. If these have all been successful, then both horse and rider should be in a good position to attempt flying change.

The trainer must decide on which rein the horse prefers to canter, as this is the rein to which we are going to attempt to change. For the purpose of this lesson we will assume that the horse prefers to canter to the left. We put him into canter right, make half a circuit of the school and change the rein, say, from K to M. As the student crosses the X marker he is asked to 'forget that you are in canter, think of yourself as being in sitting trot, and in the corner after M, canter left'. If the preparatory work has been correct and the student applies the aid correctly, the horse will make the flying change.

This may seem an oversimplification, but it has several distinct advantages:

a. It discourages the student rider from making too much preparation.
b. Until the rider becomes really quite advanced he will find it difficult to try to co-ordinate the application of the canter leg aids with the footfalls of the horse, so to think of making the flying change as making canter from trot may be helpful.
c. It may help the rider as the horse is mechanically encouraged to change in the corner from counter canter on the leg that he finds least comfortable to canter on the leg which he finds easier.

The disadvantages of making the flying change in this way are:

a. The horse may learn to anticipate the change and disobediently change each time he enters a corner in counter canter. This often results in the horse changing only in front which can be a very troublesome problem.

b. It involves both horse and rider in a double task of riding the corner correctly and the problems of making the change.

The second method The rider makes a 15m circle in canter off the track from the half marker, and a smooth angle back to the track to change leg as the horse reaches it on his new rein. It is based on the principle that the horse will want to change from counter canter on the leading leg that he enjoys least, to true canter on the leading leg that he enjoys most. The preparatory work and warming up should be the same as for the first method.

Having made two or three complete 15m circles from the half marker in canter on the rein that the horse least enjoys, the rider is then asked to make a half circle and a smooth angle back to the track to join it before reaching the quarter marker. He should then be asked to walk as he reaches the track, and after two or three steps, to strike off in canter on his new rein. Having made this simple change on rejoining the track two or three times, he can then be told again to think that he is in sitting trot as he makes his angle back to the track, and as he reaches it to apply the aids to canter on his new rein, so making the flying change. The disadvantage of this method is that, once again, the flying change is involved with a change of direction which may lead to problems when making a series of tempo changes which must be on a straight line.

The third method This may be considered to be, classically, the most correct. Here the rider is asked to work on a large circle to the left or to the right. He makes frequent transitions from walk to canter to walk, remaining on the large circle and making the strike-off both to the left and to the right. The number of steps in both walk and canter should be varied, as should the direction of the strike-off.

Having established good quality walk-to-canter and canter-to-walk transitions on the circle, the number of steps in walk can be reduced until the horse is making flying change in response to the canter aids from right to left or from left to right. Once again, success in this exercise is more likely if the horse is asked to change from counter canter to canter on the rein which he finds easier.

The advantage of this method is that the horse is being asked to change his canter lead entirely by the correct use of the aids, and there is no reliance on either the change of direction, or the horse feeling that 'here is a logical place to change the lead', both of which introduce an element of disobedience. An added advantage is that both rider and trainer have an unlimited number of opportunities to ask for the change, and this enables the rider to give the aid when he feels that the horse is ready, rather than at any particular part of the school. The instructor must be very careful not to go on with this exercise for too long, particularly if tension and anticipation is building up in the horse.

As a general rule, all work should be carried out equally on both reins. However, if both horse and rider are new to this work, the easier change must be worked on until it can be performed confidently and calmly. The change in the opposite direction can then be introduced.

Where the horse is making this work for the first time, he must be adequately rewarded after one change, and the rider should change the exercise or dismount and finish for that day. This work is physically demanding on the horse and should not be continued for more than a few days before different work is introduced for variety.

Pirouettes

a. The pirouette (half-pirouette) is a circle (half-circle), executed on two tracks, with a radius equal to the length of the horse, and the forehand moving round the haunches.

b. Pirouettes (half-pirouettes) are usually carried out at a collected walk or canter, but can also be executed at piaffe.

c. At the pirouette (half-pirouette) the fore feet and the outside hind foot move round the inside hind foot, which forms the pivot and should return to the same spot, or slightly in front of it each time it leaves the ground.

d. At whatever pace the pirouettes (half-pirouettes) are executed, the horse, slightly bent to the direction in which he is turning, should remain 'on the bit' with a light contact and turn smoothly round, maintaining the exact rhythm and sequence of footfalls in that pace.

e. During the pirouettes (half-pirouettes) the horse should maintain his impulsion, and never move backwards or deviate sideways. If the inside hind foot is not raised and returned to the ground in the same rhythm as the outside hind foot, the pace is no longer regular.

f. The quality of the pirouettes (half-pirouettes) is judged according to the suppleness, lightness, cadence and regularity of the movement, and to the precision and smoothness of the transitions; pirouettes (half-pirouettes) at canter are also judged according to the balance, the elevation and the number of strides used. Ideally a pirouette should be executed in 6–8 strides, and a half-pirouette in 3–4 strides.

The walk pirouette The pirouette in walk is a turn on the haunches in which the horse pivots around his inside hind foot whilst maintaining the regular, even, four-time tempo of his walk. Any loss of this tempo is a serious fault.

The pirouette is made in collected walk and is best introduced to both horse and rider by making a 6m volte in walk. The aids for making this volte are exactly the same as the aids for making any other circle. As the horse improves in making the volte, the size can be decreased until the horse can make the first quarter of the volte into a quarter-pirouette (Fig 41). This is achieved by the rider slightly varying the blend of the volte aids: the inside hand now has to invite the horse round on a shorter route, the outside hand prevents him from walking forwards on the circle, the outside leg acts as the quarter controlling leg and asks the quarters to come round, whilst the inside leg remains at the girth to maintain the impulsion and to prevent the horse from stepping backwards.

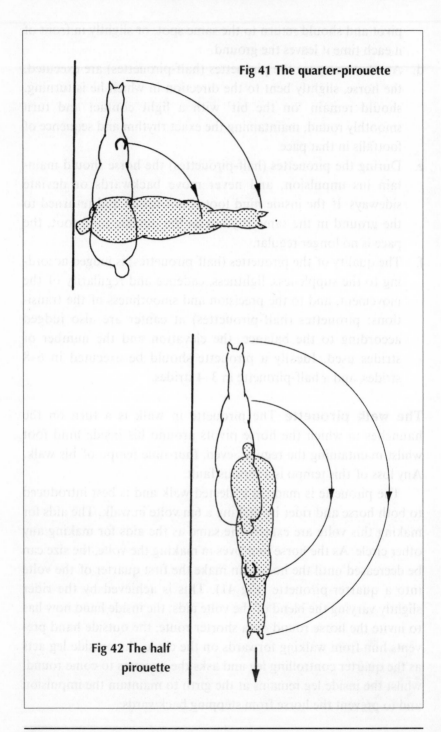

Fig 41 The quarter-pirouette

Fig 42 The half pirouette

Having completed the quarter-pirouette the horse should be ridden energetically forward in walk. Once the quarter-pirouette has been mastered successfully the pupil can then go on to making a half-pirouette by continuing to apply the same aids (Fig 42).

The canter pirouette This is a very advanced exercise and must not be attempted until the horse can work quietly and calmly in canter with a very high degree of collection. He must be able, whilst maintaining the clear three-time rhythm, to slow the canter steps right down until he is almost cantering on the spot, but keeping good impulsion.

There are a number of important factors to bear in mind when teaching this exercise:

a. The rider must maintain a correct, upright, balanced position.
b. The work is very tiring on the horse and should not be overdone.
c. The full pirouette should be built up through the quarter-, the half- and the three-quarter pirouette.
d. It is a great advantage if the rider can be trained first on a horse that will perform this exercise well when the correct aids are applied.

As in all advanced work this exercise can be introduced to the horse and rider in a number of ways, and it is for the trainer to decide which of these approaches is best for a particular pupil.

1. Whilst making a large pirouette in walk the horse can be asked to strike off in canter, make two or three steps in canter pirouette and then be sent straight forwards in canter. If the balance is lost or the work deteriorates the horse should be returned to walk and sent straight forwards. The walk-to-canter strike-off must be of high quality if this method is to be successful.
2. A small half circle of about 6m is made in collected canter at the end of the long side of the school. The horse is then ridden down the long side in renvers and the half-pirouette is made towards the wall. This method is particularly useful if the

hindquarters have been swinging out in previous attempts, a frequent difficulty in this exercise.

3. It is sometimes helpful to make a few steps in canter pirouette from a good half-pass as the bend should be correct, the collection good and the outside hind leg well engaged.

4. The canter pirouette can be made eventually on a straight line, when a degree of success has been achieved with one or more of the previous methods. Just before the point at which the pirouette or half-pirouette is to be made, the horse should be put into a degree of shoulder-in to correct the bend, control the shoulders, and help achieve sufficient collection.

Piaffe

The piaffe is a highly measured, collected, elevated and cadenced trot on the spot. The horse's back is supple and vibrating. The quarters are slightly lowered, the haunches with active hocks are well engaged giving great freedom, lightness and mobility to the shoulders and forehand. Each diagonally opposed pair of feet is raised and returned to the ground alternately, with an even rhythm and a slightly prolonged suspension.

In principle, the height of the toe of the raised foreleg should be level with the middle of the canon bone of the other foreleg. The toe of the raised hindleg should reach just above the fetlock joint of the other hindleg.

Teaching the piaffe to horse and rider is a task for the experienced trainer only. The exercise is the culmination of maximum impulsion and lightness of the forehand. When the horse is capable of a high degree of collection and can make the transitions from collected trot to halt, and collected trot to working trot smoothly, combined with the ability to make collected walk whilst remaining straight and calm, piaffe can be attempted.

It should first be made in hand with the horse dressed as for lungeing with the side-reins sufficiently short to prevent him bending his neck too much to the left or the right when in his collected outline. To start with, this training is best carried out on the track with the horse parallel to the wall.

Fig 43 Piaffe: a highly collected, elevated and cadenced trot performed almost on the spot

When working on the left rein the trainer holds the lunge rein with his left hand and a long whip (not a lungeing whip) in his right hand. The horse is worked in collected walk and the speed gradually reduced by the use of the lunge rein which is held up fairly close to the lunge cavesson. The impulsion is maintained by the trainer tapping the horse lightly below the hocks with the long whip. As soon as one or two steps are made in piaffe, whilst still moving slightly forwards, the horse is allowed to go forwards and is rewarded by a pat on the neck. The exercise should be made with frequent changes of rein.

Once the piaffe is becoming established in hand, it can be attempted with the rider in the saddle. The work is once again made from collected walk, the rider slowing down the speed with the fingers and maintaining the impulsion with his seat and legs. The trainer may still help from the ground by tapping the hindlegs alternately just below the hocks in rhythm with the steps. It is very important at this stage that the horse is allowed to go forwards a little as he makes piaffe. Only in the most advanced tests is piaffe required on the spot. It is always better if the horse is going forwards a little; he must *never* step back.

Passage

This is a measured, very collected, very elevated and very cadenced trot. It is characterised by a pronounced engagement of the quarters, a more accentuated flexion of the knees and hocks, and a graceful elasticity of movement. Each diagonally opposed pair of feet is raised and returned to the ground alternately, with an even rhythm and a prolonged suspension. In principle the height of the toe of the raised foreleg should be level with the middle of the canon bone of the other foreleg. The toe of the raised hindleg should be slightly above the fetlock joint of the other hindleg.

The neck should be raised and gracefully arched with the poll as the highest point and the head close to the perpendicular. The horse should remain light and 'on the bit' and should go smoothly from the passage to the piaffe and vice versa, with no apparent effort and without altering the rhythm. The impulsion should always be lively and pronounced.

Irregular steps with the hindlegs and swinging the forehand or the quarters from one side to the other are both serious faults.

This is a very advanced exercise and is probably the ultimate test of the rider's 'feel' and the correct logical training of his horse. If the horse is working well in piaffe and is willing to go freely forwards from it, the rider should not find a few steps in passage too difficult. The horse is sent energetically forwards from piaffe by the rider's seat and legs, with the hands allowing him to go forwards but at the same time restraining the movement sufficiently to produce the graceful, elevated steps of passage.

It must be remembered that passage requires great physical effort from the horse and only a few steps should be asked for at first. On completion of the few steps in passage the horse should be ridden forwards in collected trot to ensure that this does not deteriorate as a result of the introduction of passage.

OTHER SCHOOLING EXERCISES
NOT INCLUDED IN THE DRESSAGE TEST

Turn on the forehand

This is a controversial exercise used by some trainers to improve the horse's co-ordination and to encourage him to move away from the rider's leg. It is often used as a fundamental introduction to lateral work. It can be made in two ways, firstly with the horse looking away from the direction in which he is turning; and secondly, with the horse looking towards the way he is turning. Turn on the forehand is made from the halt, which encourages those who are opposed to it, to say that it is an exercise made without impulsion, and which therefore puts unnecessary strain on the fetlock joints of the forelegs.

To perform the exercise correctly, the horse is brought to the halt on the inside track square and on the bit. If he is to turn to the

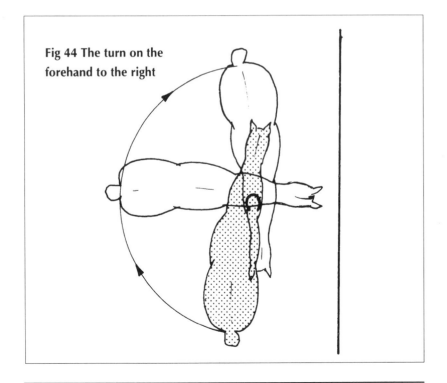

Fig 44 The turn on the forehand to the right

right, he is bent a little in that direction with the right hand, and the right leg drawn back behind the girth then asks him to move his hindquarters round with regular, even steps. The left hand prevents him from moving forwards, and the left leg is kept in contact to prevent him from stepping back (Fig 44). The aids for a turn on the forehand to the left are the reverse of those used for a turn to the right. On completion of the turn the horse should be ridden forwards with impulsion. As he pivots around the inside fore foot in this exercise, it should be used in moderation, to avoid putting too great a strain on the fetlock joint. A further disadvantage is that it may encourage the horse to come on to his forehand.

There is a similar exercise, sometimes called the 'turn about the forehand', in which the horse walks a small circle with his fore feet and a larger circle with his hind feet to make a 180 degree turn. This is somewhat more acceptable in that it can be made with impulsion and the four-time tempo of the walk can be maintained.

The half-halt

This exercise entails re-balancing the horse before attempting a transition or any dressage movement. It consists of checking his speed with the fingers of the outside hand whilst maintaining the impulsion with the inside leg or the leg and the seat. It is an important exercise which should be taught to all riders, and its importance should be thoroughly understood by those who train competition riders.

6

TEACHING THE RIDER
TO JUMP

Jumping technique as we know it today is a direct result of the thoughts and work of Captain Frederico Caprilli who was the Riding Master at the Italian Cavalry School at the turn of the century. Before that time it was usual for the rider to lean back when jumping, thereby in fact preventing the horse from using himself to the best of his ability.

Caprilli saw how vital it was for the horse to have the full use of his head, neck and back to be able to jump and go fast across country. He therefore devised a style of riding in which the rider leaned forwards to take the weight directly off the horse's back and moved his hands forwards to allow the horse to balance himself. Whilst Caprilli personally did not incline the top part of his body as far forwards as riders do today, he was the instigator of what was to become known as the 'forward seat'.

The principles for jumping are exactly the same as they are for riding on the flat: the horse must go forwards calmly, keeping a straight line, and the rider must be balanced, still and correct in his riding position.

When jumping, the rider is asked to shorten his stirrups two or three holes from his flatwork length. This enables him to incline the top part of his body forwards, which he needs to do to stay in balance with his horse. When deciding how much to shorten the stirrups it is a good guide to fit the rider's knee correctly into the knee roll of the jumping saddle. If the saddle is the correct size for the rider this should give him the correct length of stirrup leather.

The instructor must also take into account the rider's length of leg, and must use his discretion to assess the correct length for each pupil.

Once again it is very much to the rider's advantage if he can start his jumping on a 'schoolmaster' horse before he attempts to jump a young or untrained horse. Learning on an experienced horse that will approach the fence calmly and in a well balanced manner, taking regular, even strides, will give the pupil confidence and will help him achieve the correct mental and physical approach.

Before the pupil is introduced to jumping he must have an independent seat. This means he should be able to walk, trot and canter on a trained horse, maintaining his balance by a correct yet supple position, thereby leaving his legs and hands free to apply the aids. He should also have been trained in all three paces over undulating country and should be able to ride confidently at each pace without stirrups.

STARTING JUMP TRAINING

The training should start with the pupil trotting over poles on the ground, placed about 137cm (4ft 6in) apart for a 16hh horse. Three or five poles are better than two, four or six poles, as the horse is less likely to attempt to jump poles two at a time if there is an odd number. The rider is asked to trot through the poles at working trot rising, maintaining the correct tempo and speed. When he has established this and can remain in balance throughout, a jump or cavaletti at about 40cm (1ft 4in) high can be introduced 3m (9ft 10in) from the last trotting pole (Fig 45). The rider is then asked to come through the trotting poles again and over the small jump, making sure that he stays inclined a little bit forwards from the hips, keeps his leg still and in the correct position, and looks straight ahead maintaining a sure, but 'allowing' rein contact.

It is sometimes an advantage to fit a neckstrap to the horse so that the rider can hold it if he feels he is going to be left behind when the horse jumps. If, however, the horse is suitable and the

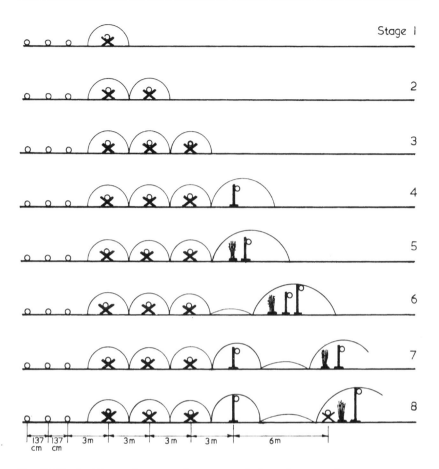

Fig 45 The build-up of progressive gymnastic jumping exercises

rider has achieved the standard of riding already described, the neckstrap should not be necessary.

Once the pupil has successfully negotiated the trotting poles and one cavaletti, a second cavaletti can be added 6m (19ft 8in) from the first. The pupil will then have to trot through the poles, jump the first cavaletti, take one stride in canter and jump the second cavaletti.

The object of this type of jumping training is to build up the rider's agility and confidence progressively until he can go forwards in balance with his horse on the approach to the jump, on take-off, over the jump and on landing. Throughout these exercises the rider must be encouraged to sit still, maintaining a sure, steady, even rein contact and with a still, quiet leg. He must be ready at any stage to apply the aids with the legs and seat or hands as required.

The exercise can be continued by increasing the number of cavaletti after the trotting poles, and varying the distance between them so that the horse takes one canter stride between them or jumps straight in and out with no canter stride. This variation in the exercise improves the co-ordination, agility and confidence of both horse and rider.

The next stage is to replace the last cavaletti by a small spread fence about 50cm (1ft 8in) in height. Once the rider's position has been established over the line of cavaletti in canter, he should be able to negotiate the small fence on the end without his position, or his rein and leg contact being upset. There is a danger here in that the rider, particularly if he has some previous jumping experience, may feel that he must make some special effort over the last jump and kick hard with his legs, drive with his seat, flap his elbows, make an exaggerated dive forwards with the upper part of his body or a combination of any of these activities which, of course, frustrates the whole object of this system of jumping training. He must therefore be warned that no extra effort is required over the last jump and that the whole purpose of the exercise is that he should establish his still, quiet position over the trotting poles and cavaletti and *maintain it* over the last jump.

The exercise can be made more demanding by replacing the cavaletti with small, varied jumps. Cross-poles, a small brush or wall, a staircase or spread fence will add variety and introduce the rider to the types of obstacle that he will have to jump singly later. The fences used must always be inviting and the distances between them correct. Nothing must ever be introduced that discourages the horse from going freely forwards in a good rhythm.

Once the rider can negotiate a line of trotting poles and cavaletti or small jumps he can attempt to negotiate a small single fence from canter. The siting of the fence and its construction should be carefully considered. The fence should preferably be placed alongside

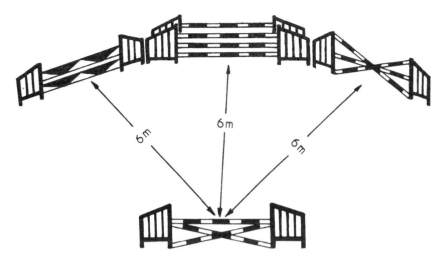

Fig 46 A useful jumping exercise

the riding school wall or another fence to encourage the horse to go straight on the approach. To assist the horse to approach the fence on a good stride it should be built carefully on the track so that the rider, having ridden a correct corner of the school or manège, will reach the jump on an accurate stride. Assuming that the rider makes a quarter of a 15m circle at canter through the corner, the jump should be about 22.5m (74ft) from the corner to allow the horse to take five canter strides before reaching the jump. To make absolutely certain of the strides approaching and including the take-off, a pole can be placed on the ground 3m (9ft 10in) in front of the jump to help both horse and rider to see and feel the point of take-off. The jump itself should be inviting with substantial wings, for example a small brush at about 60cm (2ft) with a pole above it at about 75cm (2ft 5in) and a second pole to produce a spread of about 60cm (2ft).

The rider should be told to approach the fence in exactly the same way as he rode down the line of cavaletti, sitting still, maintaining his position, feeling the rhythm of the horse's stride, keeping a definite contact with his legs and a sure but 'allowing' contact with his hands.

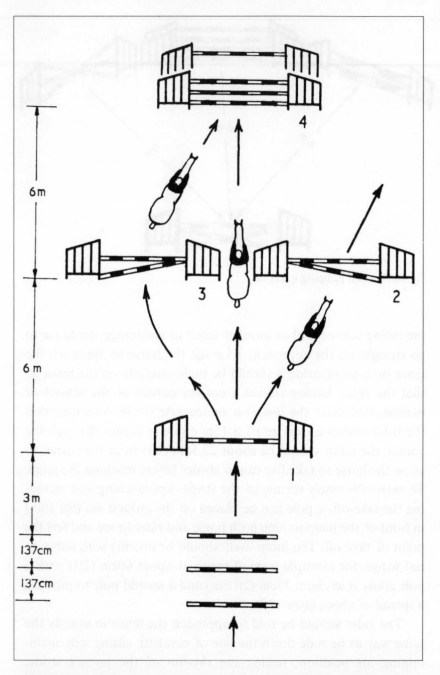

Fig 47 A gymnastic jumping exercise involving a one-stride double and changes of direction

There is a variation to this style in which the rider, with a rather longer stirrup leather, approaches the fence in an upright position and is very quick to get forward on take-off and is rather more upright as the horse lands. This style has been developed for very competent riders, riding strong, fit horses with well established, round outlines. It is particularly effective over very big fences in a small, indoor arena, where maximum control and balance are required. This technique is a refinement of the basic jumping technique and it should not be introduced to the novice jumping rider until he has mastered and is experienced in the more elementary style of jumping.

There is no doubt that whilst both riders and horses must train over jumps and courses similar to those that they are likely to meet in competition, their gymnastic jumping training is a most important part of their preparation. A number of these exercises can be prepared before the lesson begins so that both horse and rider, having warmed up, can go straight on without a long delay whilst jumps are erected (as shown in Fig 46).

The two following groups of exercises have proved useful and convenient:

Exercises group 1

The equipment is set out as in Fig 47. There are three trotting poles 137cm (4ft 6in) apart and a gap of 3m (9ft 10in) before the first jump which is a single pole at about 61cm (2ft). Jumps 2 and 3 are more single poles about 1m (3ft 3in) apart or with enough room for a horse to pass between the inside wing stands. The fourth jump is an oxer fence about 76cm (2ft 6in) high with a 76cm (2ft 6in) spread, with the back pole one hole higher than the front pole.

- The first exercise is for the rider to approach in trot through the trotting poles, jump fence number 1, make three strides in canter, pass between jumps 2 and 3 and jump fence number 4. The emphasis should be on correct riding throughout, with the horse going forwards straight and calmly with good rhythm and balance.
- In the second exercise the rider approaches on the right rein,

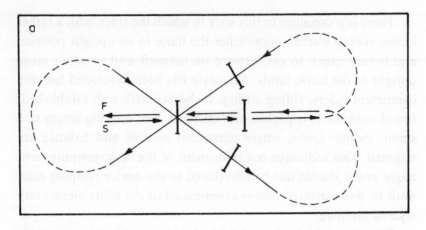

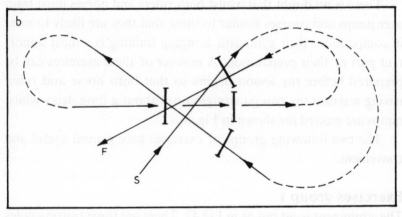

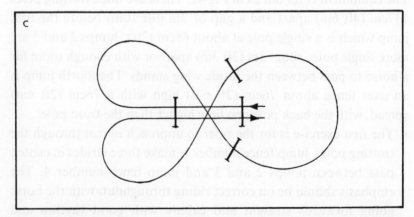

Fig 48 Gymnastic jumping exercises involving a change of rein to the right and to the left

through the trotting poles, over fence number 1, makes one stride in canter and jumps fence number 2.

- In the third exercise the rider approaches on the left rein, trots through the trotting poles, jumps fence number 1, makes one stride in canter and jumps fence number 3.

The trainer must pay particular attention to the quality of the work between these exercises. Having jumped fences 1 and 2, the rider must quickly but calmly and correctly return to trot to resume the exercise. He must not be allowed to be slack or careless between exercises.

- Exercises 4 and 5 take exercises 2 and 3 a stage further in that the rider is asked to go left after fence 2 or right after fence 3, take one stride in canter and jump fence 4. It must be made quite clear to the rider that he must only go on to fence 4 if he is in control and can jump the fence in a calm and balanced way. If it is going to involve a struggle in any way he must ride away and re-establish his control and balance before attempting to jump.

Exercises group 2

The jumps for these exercises can be set up before the lesson starts, leaving the track free for warming up and other preparatory work. Fig 48 shows the layout of the fences. There are, of course, many types that can be utilised, but it should be remembered that all the fences must be built to be jumped in both directions, and a selection of tracks should be ridden to give this exercise variety (Figs 48a, b, c).

Whilst the instructor must pay attention to the actual jumping in this exercise, it is particularly useful for students being trained to ride correctly between fences, maintaining their balance, bend, control, calmness and impulsion. It teaches the pupil to use the arena correctly and to full advantage, and to plan ahead.

Further training to improve the jumping rider

Having established a degree of confidence and competence in the rider which enables him to jump a course of small fences up to 1m (3ft 3in) high, the trainer must then go on to teach him:

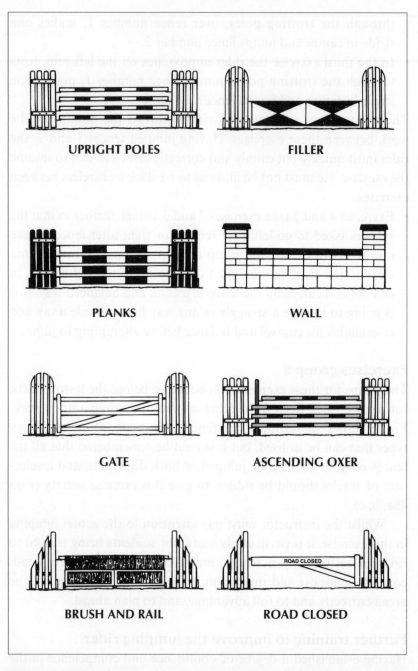

UPRIGHT POLES

FILLER

PLANKS

WALL

GATE

ASCENDING OXER

BRUSH AND RAIL

ROAD CLOSED

Fig 49 The different types of fence which might be used in a showjumping course

a. How to walk a course, either in showjumping or cross-country.
b. How to ride a course of jumps at a required speed.
c. How to cope with jumps of different types.

Further training must then include gymnastic work that will improve his confidence, agility, balance, grip and fitness, all of which will be needed at some stage in the 'rough and tumble' of competition riding.

WALKING THE JUMPING COURSE

Training here must include:
a. Reading the schedule and knowing the conditions of the competition, such as the speed and the table under which it is being held.
b. Studying the course plan, taking particular note of the location of the start and finish and any obligatoirs through which the rider must pass.
c. Allowing enough time to walk the course without being rushed. It may be necessary on occasions to walk it a second or third time.
d. Careful study of the line that the rider intends to take, paying particular attention to where he can take short-cuts, the stretches on which he may be able to make up time, and those where he must go slowly.
e. The way the rider intends to jump each individual fence, with special attention as to what he will do where there is a choice of routes. Here he should consider what to do in the event of a refusal at his first choice, as it may be sensible to take an easier route than to risk a second refusal.
f. The measurement of the distances between combination fences. He must learn to pace out the distance between fences so that he knows exactly how many strides his horse will take between them and how he will have to influence these strides.

RIDING A COURSE AT A REQUIRED SPEED

A competition course invariably has to be ridden at a specified number of metres per minute, the pace being slower for novice competitions and faster for more advanced competitions.

It is important that the competition rider is trained to ride at the speed demanded by the rules. It is infuriating to incur unnecessary time faults, but it is also wasteful to ride the horse too fast, particularly if there are further phases of the competition for which the horse will require maximum energy. Training to ride a showjumping course in the required time is largely a matter of practice, and will improve with experience and knowledge of the horse's capabilities.

Horse trials: roads and tracks

When riding the roads and tracks phases of a horse trial the rider must be trained to use his watch, paying particular attention to the kilometre markers en route. Some trainers and riders find it useful to write the check times, by kilometre markers, on a card which is taped to the rider's forearm. This enables the competitor to check whether he is up or down on his time schedule.

The steeplechase

For the steeplechase phase the competitor must learn to gallop at 690m (2,264ft) per minute. This is not particularly fast, but the trainer must find a way to help his rider to assess the correct speed, avoiding time faults or taking too much out of his horse. Several racecourses have facilities for motor cars to be driven alongside the actual track outside the rail. If permission can be obtained to gallop on one of these from time to time, it is very convenient for the trainer to drive alongside his galloping pupil setting the exact speed.

The cross-country

Riding the cross-country phase at the correct speed is largely a matter of experience again, but when training at home some time must be spent on riding across varying terrain and jumping fences at the speed required under the supervision of the trainer with a stopwatch. Interval training can play an important part in teaching the rider pace judgement. An important point that appears to be overlooked by many trainers is that where riders are required to carry extra weight in competition to meet a minimum weight requirement, this weight (or at least some of it) should be carried in training. It is a serious mistake to leave the carrying of the extra weight until the day of the competition.

COPING WITH JUMPS OF VARIOUS TYPES

The rider must be trained to vary his approach to particular fences in order to cope with the problems set by the different designs. For example, the steeplechase fence is thick and slopes away with a good groundline, and is generally inviting, and the horse can brush through the top 25cm (10in) or so; it can therefore be approached on a good long stride at the gallop. On the other hand, a stile is narrow, upright and with no groundline or wings and so will require a more accurate approach and more precise jumping.

These are the two extremes, and there are many other types of fence and approach which need careful consideration. Jumping up and down hill, into and out of water, up and down banks and drops all need to be carefully studied. Combination fences often cause problems to both horse and rider. The jumping trainer must school his pupils over combination fences, varying the number of strides between the elements, the number of elements in the combination and the design of each one. He must never set distances between fences which are incorrect, or discourage the horse from attempting to jump the combination with confidence.

A guide to recommended distances in combination fences is shown in Figs 50a and b.

Fig 50 A guide to recommended distances in combination jumping:
(a) Suitable distances for horse; (b) Suitable distances for ponies
(Reproduced by kind permission of the British Show Jumping Association)

A guide to recommended distances in combination jumping
(a) Suitable distance for horses
For combination obstacles the following average distances are suggested
for horses according to the type of obstacles included in the combination

→	A	B	C	D
E	7.30m to 7.90m	7.15m to 7.60m	7.00m to 7.60m	6.85m to 7.45m
	(24'0" to 26'0")	(23'6" to 25'0")	(23'0" to 25'0")	(22'6" to 24'6")
	10.50m to 10.95m	10.50m to 10.80m	10.35m to 10.80m	10.00m to 10.50m
	(34'6" to 36'0")	(34'6" to 35'6")	(34'0" to 35'6")	(33'0" to 34'6")
F	7.45m to 7.75m	7.00m to 7.30m	6.85m to 7.30m	6.70m to 7.30m
	(24'6" to25'6")	(23'0" to 24'0")	(22'6" to 24'0")	(22'0" to 24'0")
	10.50m to 10.80m	10.35m to 10.65m	10.00m to 10.65m	10.00m to 10.20m
	(34'6" to 35'6")	(34'0" to 35'0")	(33'0" to 35'0")	(33'0" to 33'6")
G	7.45m to 7.90m	7.00m to 7.45m	6.85m to 7.45m	6.85m to 7.30m
	(24'6" to 26'0")	(23'0" to 24'6")	(22'6" to 24'6")	(22'6" to 24'0")
	10.50m to 10.95m	10.35m to 10.80m	10.20m to 10.80m	10.00m to 10.50m
	(34'6" to 36'0")	(34'0" to 35'6")	(33'6" to 35'6")	(33'0" to 34'6")
H	7.60m to 8.00m	7.45m to 7.60m	7.30m to 7.60m	6.85m to 7.30m
	(25'0" to 26'6")	(24'6" to 25'0")	(24'0" to 25'0")	(22'6" to 24'0")
	10.80m to 11.10m	10.65m to 10.95m	10.50m to 10.80m	10.00m to 10.35m
	(35'6" to 36'6")	(35'0" to 36'0")	(34'6" to 35'6")	(33'0" to 34'0")

(b) Suitable distances for ponies
Suggested distances for 14.2hh ponies. It is suggested for 12.2hh and 13.2hh ponies that the distances below be reduced by 15cm in a one stride combination and 30cm in a two stride combination
Because a pony's stride varies so much, it is safer NOT to have a spread in the middle or at the end of a combination of a one stride distance

	ONE STRIDE			TWO STRIDES		
	Minimum distance	Maximum to a spread	Max to a vertical	Minimum distance	Maximum to a spread	Max to a vertical
128cms (12.2hh)	5.95m (19ft 6in	Not allowed	6.55m (21ft 6in)	8.55m (28ft)	9.45m (31ft)	9.75m (32ft)
138cms (13.2hh)	6.25m (20ft 6in	Not allowed	7.00m (23ft)	9.15m (30ft)	9.90m (32ft 6in)	10.20m (33ft 6in)
148cms (14.2hh)	6.55m (21ft 6in	7.15m (23ft 6in)	7.45m (24ft 6in)	9.60m (31ft 6in)	10.20m (33ft 6in)	10.65m (35ft)

GYMNASTIC JUMPING TRAINING FOR THE RIDER

Work without stirrups will improve the rider's balance and confidence. Also a certain amount of rising trot without stirrups will improve his grip, and strengthen and condition the leg muscles. However, this training should be watched very carefully by the instructor because, although it is very beneficial to the jumping rider, it may spoil his seat and position on the flat should he begin to grip up excessively.

Gymnastic jumping without stirrups down a lane of cavaletti or jumps, and later with the reins knotted and the rider's arms folded, will all help to build a confident, fit and agile competition rider.

All competitors should learn to spring into the saddle from the ground without the use of the stirrups. Valuable seconds are often lost after a fall in a competition when the rider cannot vault quickly into the saddle.

To compete successfully the rider must be physically fit. The sight of a horse in a three-day event or a point-to-point which is fitter than his rider is not uncommon but is, of course, quite unacceptable to the riding trainer. At the end of a hard race or a testing cross-country course a fit rider can be of considerable help to his horse, whilst the unfit rider is a positive handicap. It is the duty of the trainer therefore to ensure that both horse and rider are sufficiently fit to put into practice in competition everything that they have learned in training. Running or cycling and a few suppling exercises should be part of the daily programme of all competition riders, be they concerned in eventing, showjumping, dressage or racing.

7

CLASSROOM TEACHING

Most riding instructors are at home in the riding school whether indoors or outside: this is the environment in which they have been trained and the workshop in which they pursue their chosen sport.

The complete riding instructor must be able to teach not only in the riding school but in the classroom as well – although this is a prospect which fills most junior and some senior instructors with horror. But this fear is quite unfounded because, by observing a few simple rules, classroom teaching can be a most rewarding and interesting challenge.

PREPARING A LESSON

The following factors should therefore be considered when preparing a lesson:

- The aim: the instructor must first define the aim of his lesson. It must be clear, simple and practicable – but before it can be considered practicable it must be related to:
- The time available for the lesson: how long is it?
- The class: how many pupils are there? How much do they know already? How quickly can they learn?

Having decided on the aim, the subject matter can now be considered.

Subject matter The instructor must know this thoroughly and must consider carefully the information required to achieve the aim. Having decided this it must be grouped under subject headings.

Ways of presentation Different ways will suggest themselves. The most suitable way for the subject must be selected.

Training aids The parts of the lesson which require reinforcing with illustrations or training aids should be considered.

Conditions of work Is a classroom needed? Will the tackroom or feedroom do?

Successful instruction is based on the common sense and imaginative use of the following principles and techniques.

The principles
Preparation and planning.
Promotion and the maintenance of the desire to learn.
Confirmation that instruction has been learned.

The techniques
Question technique.
The use of training aids.

These principles and techniques should not be treated in isolation; they are closely related and should be combined to achieve the best results possible.

PREPARATION AND PLANNING

Any lesson or lecture must be planned so that the various phases of instruction are presented logically and progressively. The lesson should be divided into three phases:

The beginning
Preliminaries Anything which cannot be done until the class assembles, such as giving out equipment, roll call, etc.

Revision Where there is a link with a previous lesson, a short time should be spent on revision. This provides a good base on which to start the lesson and attunes the pupils' minds to the subject to be covered.

Introduction At this stage the instructor is able to introduce the subject and achieve the interest of his class by stating the aim clearly, and providing an incentive to learn where possible.

The middle

This part of the lesson contains the main teaching. The subject matter must be divided into groups and the instructor must carefully eliminate anything which is either irrelevant or unnecessary. What remains must then be carefully arranged in logical order and at the end of each stage the instructor must confirm by question and answer technique that what he has taught has been absorbed by his class.

The end

To finish the lesson neatly the instructor should confirm that the class has understood what has been taught. This should be done by allowing questions from the class to enable them to clear up any doubts that may exist and by putting questions to the class or arranging a short test or quiz.

Finally, he should sum up to emphasise the major points of the lesson, and include a 'look forward' to the subject of the next lesson in order to arouse interest in it.

PROMOTION AND MAINTENANCE OF THE DESIRE TO LEARN

As a rule, people who come to an instructor to learn equitation and its related subjects do so because they have a real interest in the horse. For classroom instruction to be successful, however, interest in the subject must be stimulated.

Firstly, the class should be given something to look forward to in their next lesson. When running a course of instruction pupils should be given an interesting and attractively laid out written pro-gramme so that they know exactly what to expect at any particular period. Advertising the lesson can be of help; any display which will arouse curiosity will promote interest in the subject.

Once the lesson has started, the introduction should include:

- A clear statement of what is to be learned.
- A realistic reason why this subject is important, and why it should be learned.
- Whether or not there is any reward to be gained from knowledge of the subject.

The enthusiasm of the instructor will play a major part in main-taining the pupils' interest throughout the lesson, and the good instructor will involve them in as much activity as possible: mental activity when teaching facts, and physical activity when teaching skills.

As many of the students' senses as possible should be involved. Hearing is most frequently involved in teaching, in that most instructors rely on speech to put their subjects across. Talking can be monotonous, however, and the dreary voice of many teachers has often sent the most enthusiastic student to sleep. The involve-ment of the class in touching, seeing, smelling and tasting, where applicable, will promote class activity and maintain lively interest. To give a simple example: it would be very difficult to teach a pupil to tie a bow tie by just describing it to him verbally, and much more effective to show him how it is done and then to give him a bow tie to practise by himself under the instructor's guidance.

Instruction must be as realistic as possible. For instance, when teaching a pupil the principles of assessing the age of a horse by examination of the teeth, much can be done in the classroom, but the pupil must at some stage look into the mouth of a real horse to examine the teeth and complete this study.

Instruction must be related to everyday life, and it is important that the instructor relates his teaching to practical situations that will be encountered by his pupils.

Interest can also be maintained by the use of clear and imaginative training aids such as films, slides, posters, the overhead projector, etc. These will be discussed later.

CONFIRMATION THAT INSTRUCTION HAS BEEN LEARNED

The instructor must ensure that, as far as possible, the teaching has been absorbed and understood. The lesson must therefore develop in logical and limited stages towards the final aim, and the instructor should confirm that each stage has been thoroughly understood before he continues to the next.

At the end of the lesson both the instructor and the class will want to know how well they have done, which is best achieved by two-way questioning.

QUESTION TECHNIQUE

To maintain class interest and to involve the pupils in the work the instructor must understand:

a. The purpose of questions in teaching.
b. How to put questions to the class.
c. How to answer questions from the class.

The purpose of questioning is threefold:

a. To teach, by making the class think out the answers by themselves.
b. To involve the class by keeping them mentally active.
c. To confirm that the lesson has been absorbed and understood.

When putting a question to the class it should be directed to the whole class, a pause made to allow each pupil time to think, and then one pupil invited to answer. It is a mistake to nominate the student who is to answer *before* the question is put, because this usually leads to the rest of the class breathing a sigh of relief and giving the matter no further thought.

The instructor should ensure that the question is understood, and he must avoid ambiguity. Questions which encourage guessing are of little value, and 50/50 questions come into this category. For instance, a question that requires an answer 'yes' or 'no' or 'black' or 'white' does not really test whether or not the lesson has been learned. Questions which test a skill or the pupils' powers of expression (unless of course this is the intention) should also be avoided.

When pupils are given the opportunity to question the instructor, any question raised should be put back to the rest of the class. If the point has been generally missed it may show up a weakness in the instruction. If the question concerns a subject which is yet to be covered, the class should be told that the matter will be dealt with at a later stage. And where the question reveals a deficiency in the lesson, the instructor should take note and make the necessary corrections.

Irrelevant questions are often asked, and if the question is genuine it should be dealt with either by a brief answer or by explaining that it does not fit into that lesson and will be answered at another time. This type of questioning should not be discouraged, but a deliberate 'red herring' must be squashed promptly and effectively.

When the question is relevant but the instructor does not know the answer, it is a mistake for him to try to bluff his way out. He must admit that he does not know the answer and undertake to provide it at a later date, which obviously he must not then forget to do.

Good question technique stimulates class activity and keeps pupils alert. No one likes to look foolish but everyone enjoys answering correctly. A good question is one that the class can understand, is not ambiguous, discourages guessing and promotes thought.

Plan the questions and know the answers.

THE USE OF TRAINING AIDS

Teaching can be made clearer and simpler by the use of various training aids. These are used to help the instructor by reinforcing his teaching.

Blackboard and chalk

This equipment is cheap and simple and is available to most instructors. It is not, however, always used to the best advantage. White chalk is not always the clearest colour: yellow is often better and whilst red, blue and brown can make an interesting change and add variety, they are often difficult to see. Light shining on a blackboard can make it impossible for some of the class to see what is written.

Writing freehand on a blackboard requires practice and a little artistic flair. It is good preparation for the instructor to write on the blackboard in pencil before the class begins. The class cannot see what is written, but the instructor, standing close to the board, can see it clearly. This has several advantages: it provides him with an aide memoire, plans his writing on the blackboard, avoiding the embarrassment of running out of space, and prevents writing at an angle, mis-spelling or cramping an illustration.

Where a blackboard is to be prepared, the work will be much clearer if the chalk is first dipped in water, and as the chalk on the board dries it becomes very bright and clear. If the work on the blackboard is to be kept, the chalk can be dipped into a solution of gum arabic which will result in the work drying up bright and semi-permanent.

Posters

These can be easily and cheaply made. Chalk, felt-tipped pen or poster paint are all useful mediums used on white or coloured paper. The advantage of the poster is that it can easily be rolled up and stored until required for display.

Video tapes

Several are now available covering a wide range of subjects; they are easy to show, and the equipment needed is widely available. It must be remembered, however, that the video will only support other teaching and should not be used in isolation. Where a video is used to present a subject on its own, the teacher must allow time for it to be discussed and for the pupils to ask questions.

Slides

These are cheap, easy to show, and can be taken by an amateur photographer and used to illustrate a particular point. The apparatus required to show them is inexpensive, and they can be easily arranged to illustrate a lesson quickly and effectively.

Models

These are very useful where the real item is either unobtainable or inconvenient, for example the skeleton of the horse, a dressage arena or a showjumping course.

Specimens

Very often the best way to demonstrate is to provide the student in the classroom with a specimen of the real thing, for example a surgical shoe, samples of oats or other cereals or the farrier's tools.

Actual equipment

There are occasions when it is possible to provide the actual equipment which is the subject of the lesson in the classroom. For example, when teaching the stripping and cleaning of clippers it is clearly an advantage to have the clippers in the class and to let each of the pupils handle them.

The overhead projector

An expensive piece of equipment which will project a hand-made transparency on to a screen. The transparency can be easily made on a transparent sheet about one foot (30cm) square by writing or drawing with a felt-tipped pen. This system gives considerable scope for building up a picture on the screen by laying one transparency upon another. It is a most useful and convincing means of presentation.

Video recording

A means of recording an activity on a cassette and being able to play it back through a normal television receiver. It is expensive but is especially useful, because the pupils in the class can be recorded performing a particular task and can later watch themselves on the screen with the obvious advantage of being able to discuss the results. A further advantage is that the tape can be stopped at any time to freeze a frame and can be rewound for a particular passage to be re-shown. A sound track can also be recorded on the video cassette.

The use of training aids must always be planned. They should be kept hidden until they are required and should be removed as soon as they are finished with, otherwise they may cause distractions.

Remember that the aid is only to help the teacher to make his point: the teacher must teach, and the aid will emphasise certain aspects of the lesson.

Classrooms

Classrooms should be quiet and free from distractions. It is a mistake to have classroom walls covered with posters, no matter how attractive or interesting they are, as they cause distractions and should be avoided. Similarly, there should not be a window overlooking the manège or riding school because any student will look out of the classroom when there is something interesting to see, which again is clearly undesirable.

IN CONCLUSION

Good classroom teaching depends on preparation and planning, and the intelligent use of questions and training aids. When students fall asleep in the classroom it is always the fault of the teacher!

Appendix:

Teaching Stable Management and Horsemastership

Whilst the main purpose of this book is to assist in the teaching of riding, the student's progress will be hindered and his true potential never achieved if he is not trained in stable management and horsemastership. Equitation and horse management must be studied in parallel if the rider seriously intends to become a true horseman.

The following is a guide to the aspects of stable management and horsemastership that should be included in the rider's training at various levels.

The beginner and the novice rider

- Safety in the stable yard and when working with horses.
- Handling the horse.
- The points of the horse, and colours and markings.
- Tack and equipment; fitting, care, naming the parts.
- Watering and feeding; the basic principles of feeding the horse.
- Stable bedding and bedding down.
- Mucking-out; skipping out; care of the muck heap.
- Grooming.
- The signs of health in the horse.
- Behaviour/psychology of the horse.

The competent rider/novice competitor

- Stable routine.
- Exercising/working the horse.
- Care of the competition horse.

- Feeding the competition horse: daily requirements, feed varieties, problems related to feeding; nutrition; the digestive system; recognising good/poor quality forage; the feed room.

- Recognising soundness/unsoundness.

- The foot and shoeing: the reasons for shoeing; recognising good and bad shoeing, and when the horse needs to be shod.

- Grooming, strapping.

- Clipping.

- Stable vices.

- Travelling horses: clothing and preparation in general.

- Tack and equipment: boots, bandages, martingales, varieties of saddle, the double bridle, lungeing equipment, bits and bitting.

- Veterinary care: recognising 'off-colour', 'unwell', 'seriously ill'; when to call the veterinary surgeon; treatment of wounds; other veterinary treatment: cold hosing, poulticing, etc; taking temperature, pulse and respiratory rate; sick nursing; control of internal parasites.

- Keeping the horse at grass: turning out to, and bringing up from grass; the pasture; health hazards at grass; acreage required; fencing.

- The systems of suspension and locomotion: the skeleton and superficial muscles.

The advanced rider

- Selecting and buying horses.

- Assessing the horse's age.

- Assessing conformation as it may affect the training and performance of the competition horse.

- Training the young horse: lungeing, backing, riding away.

- Training the competition horse: basic training; getting the horse fit; interval training; maintaining fitness during the competition season.

- The administrative requirements of the competition horse.
- Shoeing: the balanced foot; good shoeing; faults in shoeing; foot correction; surgical shoeing.
- Feeding the performance horse: electrolytes; probiotics; high energy foods; problems related to high performance feeding.
- Stabling: construction, materials, design; fittings; other mechanical equipment – grooming machines, chaff cutters etc.
- Anatomy and physiology: the respiratory system; the blood circulatory system; the nervous system; the endocrine system; the skin, the eyes and the ears.
- Veterinary care of the competition horse.
- The administration of veterinary medication; methods of restraint.

INDEX